The Theology of Light and Sight

The Theology of Light and Sight

An Interfaith Perspective

EDITED BY
KENNETH L. VAUX AND K. K. YEO

WIPF & STOCK · Eugene, Oregon

THE THEOLOGY OF LIGHT AND SIGHT
An Interfaith Perspective

Copyright © 2011 Wipf and Stock Publishers. All rights reserved. Except for brief quotations in critical publications or reviews, no part of this book may be reproduced in any manner without prior written permission from the publisher. Write: Permissions, Wipf and Stock Publishers, 199 W. 8th Ave., Suite 3, Eugene, OR 97401.

Wipf & Stock
An Imprint of Wipf and Stock Publishers
199 W. 8th Ave., Suite 3
Eugene, OR 97401
www.wipfandstock.com

ISBN 13: 978-1-60899-773-2

Manufactured in the U.S.A.

I extend a heartfelt thank you to my co-editor K. K. Yeo.
Thanks also to editorial assistants Jake Weber and Melanie Baffes
and to the always-encouraging editors of Wipf & Stock,
Jim Tedrick and Christian Amondson.

Contents

Prayers for Light / ix

PART 1 SCRIPTURES AND THEOLOGY

1. Light and Sight in Interfaith Theology and Ethics / 3
   by Kenneth L. Vaux

2. From Absolute Transcendence to Light: God's Ontological Generosity / 31
   by Souleymane Bachir Diagne

3. Light and New Creation in Genesis and the Gospel of John / 39
   by K. K. Yeo

PART 2 AFRICAN AND ASIAN PERSPECTIVES

4. 'Good Religion' and the Quest for Constructive Inter-religious Dialogue / 59
   by Larry Murphy

5. Violence and Obscurity: Religious Cosmology of Seeing and Hearing in the West African Rainforest / 62
   by William Murphy

6. Light and Sight in the Hindu Tradition and the Faiths of India / 77
   by Wendy Doniger

PART 3 ARTS, FILM, AND MEDICINE

7. Light and Life: The Ministry of Vincent Van Gogh / 85
   by Kenneth L. Vaux, with Richard Vaux and Jan van Eys

8. Light and Sight in Clint Eastwood's *Gran Torino* / 102
   by Sara Anson Vaux

9. How Do I Know Thee? / 114
   by Jan van Eys, MD

10. Giving Sight to the Blind / 119
    by Kimberly Curnyn, MD

PART 4   INTERFAITH COMMUNITY

11   Interfaith Futures in Academic and Religious Communities / 137
by Phillip Amerson, Morton Schapiro, Peter Knobel, Julie Windsor Mitchell, Souleymane Bachir Diagne, Mark A. Dennis, Jr.

Contributors / 153

Prayers for Light

A JEWISH PRAYER

7 Whither shall I go from Thy spirit?
 or whither shall I flee from Thy presence?
8 If I ascend up into heaven, Thou art there;
 if I make my bed in the nether-world, behold, Thou art there.
9 If I take the wings of the morning,
 and dwell in the uttermost parts of the sea;
10 Even there would Thy hand lead me,
 and Thy right hand would hold me.
11 And if I say: 'Surely the darkness shall envelop me,
 and the light about me shall be night';
12 Even the darkness is not too dark for Thee,
 but the night shineth as the day; the darkness is even as the light.

—*Psalm 139, Hebrew Bible*

CHRISTIAN PRAYERS

Christ, as a light
    illumine and guide me.
Christ, as a shield,
    overshadow me.
Christ under me;
Christ over me;
Christ beside me
    on my left and my right.
This day be within and without me,
    lowly and meek, yet all-powerful.
Be in the heart of each to whom I speak;
    in the mouth of each who speaks unto me.
This day be within and without me,
    lowly and meek, yet all-powerful.
Christ as a light;
Christ as a shield;
Christ beside me
    on my left and my right.

—Celtic Daily Prayer:
Prayers and Readings from the Northumbria Community

Blessed are you, radiant dawn of life!

Blessed are you, O God of beginnings,
    who brought forth light from the void,
    shaped heaven and earth, sea and sky,
    and breathed life into all creation.

You made us in your likeness,
    calling us to care for each other and the world,
    and through your abounding love,
    sent your Son to be the Light of life.

Grant that we may awaken to that Light,
    that we may live as you intended us to live,
    carrying the love of your Son, Jesus Christ
        to a world in need of compassion and hope.

Let Christ's presence live through us and in us,
    becoming part of all we say and do,
    so that we, too, may be bearers of your everlasting Light.

We pray this in your holy name. Amen.

—Melanie Baffes

A MUSLIM PRAYER

Merciful God, Creator of all, Light of heavens and earth

We pray to you to grant us light

Light in our hearts so as to be open to faith in you and love of you

Light in our hearing so as to listen to one another with the spirit of openness

Light in our sights and insights so as to see truth as truth and abide by it and to see wrong as wrong and avoid it

Light all around us; on our right-hands and our left-hands, before us and behind us, above us and underneath us and make us light unto each other and unto the world at large

Our Merciful Lord: we pray to you, as we begin this blessed dialogue to bless us with your light and presence and to guide our deliberations

Aameen.

—Jamal Badawi

A Prayer at the Beginning of the Evangelical/Muslim Dialogue in Toronto, Canada on Thursday, May 13, 2010 by Jamal Badawi, a servant of Allah. This prayer was inspired by both the Qur'an, Al-Noor (The Light), 24:1–2, and by two prayers of Prophet Muhammad, peace and blessing be upon him and upon all the Prophets.

PART 1

Scriptures and Theology

1

Light and Sight in Interfaith Theology and Ethics

Kenneth L. Vaux

INTRODUCTION

Our Project Interfaith finds birth today after nearly a year of planning. We begin with a spectroscopic view of the issues explored in our inaugural workshop on Light and Sight in interfaith perspective. We seek to scope out how the One God of all Truth and Life illumines this world and its peoples of faith. If the Semitic/Hellenic faiths of Abraham—along with the cognate faiths of Africa, India, China, and other regions of the world—are theologically valid and their witness is ethically virtuous, then such biblically animated divine illumination will shine as we illumine each other, will forgive us as we forgive one another, feed us as we feed each other, and redeem us as we acknowledge and prompt redemption in one another.

We meet here in Chicago, the inaugural host city of the Council for a Parliament of the World Religions, and in Evanston, host city of the 1954 World Council of Churches whose theme was "Christ: The Light of the World." We seek to stand in that heritage in which mutual consultation and service brings radiance to this dark world as "we let our light so shine that the world may see our good works and glorify our heavenly Father" (Matt 5:16).

The workshop, like a symphony, flows in three movements. In the first movement, we seek to lay down fundamental structures, purposes, and convictions. Following this introductory essay, we will rehearse the strains of Jewish, Christian, and Muslim interfaith theologies. The Christian refrain, presented by Northwestern Medievalist Barbara Newman, gives us a window into the Christian picture of faith and devotion as depicted by Hildegard of Bingen—in her conviction that God is "Living Light." Hildegard expressed these perceptions of God in texts, songs, and artistic drawings in that age of Camelot insight and interfaith awareness. "Living Light," Newman contended, drew on biblical understanding, yes, but principally on classical, Neo-Platonic, and Aristotelian metaphysical and theological understandings of God and human life. The membrane between those two *Weltanschauungen*, of course, is very porous, especially if we define a biblical worldview in inter-Abrahamic terms.

Yohanan Petrovsky-Shtern, the Russian historian and Northwestern chair of Jewish Studies, then walked us through an advanced Yeshiva tutorial on the biblical-*Talmudic*, then *midrashic* unfolding of the motif of Divine light. His thesis—that a minor theme in J, E, D, and P—the authorial strands of Torah as understated in Heschel's first three Judaisms—biblical, rabbinic, and *Talmudic*—then becomes pronounced in Hasidic and Kabbalistic renditions of the faith. In the discussion that followed, Shtern's star light and his parlance was most illuminating—the reader will note—as he waxed lyrical on the themes of color, green in particular, in the inner sanctum of holiness.

Souleymane Bachir Diagne, one of our world's eminent philosophers of Islam and science, delighted his audience with the florid light-brilliance of Muslim theology as seen by Sufi eyes.

Movement two in this first symphony of Project Interfaith is a collage of artistic renderings ranging from ophthalmologist Kim Curnyn's moving screen of sight grounded in biblical narrative and clinical care around the world—to the challenging words about the indispensable vitalities of faith in university, seminary, and community by Northwestern President Morton Schapiro and Garrett-Evangelical President Philip Amerson—and respondents from that clergy community. Concluding the day were moving analyses of the light afforded by brush and film from *frere* Richard Vaux, a New York iconographer, and his sister-in-law, Sara Anson Vaux, whose sketch of valences of light and shadow—both in texture and theme—in Clint Eastwood's *Gran Torino* climaxed a varicolored splendor as twilight descended on day one.

Movement three: On day two, the reach of the palate extended into the African Rain Forest, reflections on the Genesis-Johannine light theology by Northwestern and Garrett scholars Bill Murphy and K.K. Yeo—followed by Wendy Doniger's masterful culminating discussion of sight (faith and natural knowledge) in Indian philosophy and religion. The Mircea Eliade Professor at the University of Chicago—author of three volumes of Hindu Penguin Classics—summarily suggested that Indian philosophy teaches us to doubt what we see, while Indian theology trains us to believe what we see. Even here in the cradle of human spirituality, we see the reciprocity and complementarity of philosophy and theology as the twin pillars of criticality and credibility. The careful reader will find in this two-day symposium a primer for and a vision into the interfaith horizon of extraordinary color and value—material and mental.

WHAT IS LIGHT?

In this symposium, and in the broader project, the first issue before us is whether Light is material (scientific), metaphoric (metaphysical), moral (ethical) or all of the above. We begin with a discussion of the theological science of light.

One of my first theological teachers was Tom Torrance. Perhaps the best class I had with him was not Systematic Theology the year I spent in Edinburgh, when Barth's *Dogmatics* started to come into English from T&T Clark—in part from Tom's able translating hand. Nor was it the junior-high class at the wee *kirk* I served as minister in Whitecraig, Midlothian. I invited Torrance to lecture to the young people one evening. He spoke on Athanasius and the Trinity to what appeared to be a raptly attentive audience. It's amazing what respect the Moderator of the Church of Scotland commands, even among teeny trainspotters. My greatest learning, though, came some years later in the three days we spent together stranded in Kennedy Airport, waiting to return to London—Torrance to Auld Reekie and me to Oxford to continue a sabbatical. The four feet of snow—drifting to more than 40 feet and covering the air terminal buildings—afforded us some wonderful conversations that were tinged by the thrill and terror of apocalyptic atmosphere toward which we both tended in our Augustinian theologies.

Before this 1983 blizzard, reenacted in 2010, Torrance had already produced fine work in theology and science. He wrote an edition of his neighbor James Clerk Maxwell's *The Dynamical Theory of the Electromagnetic Field* and its theological interpretation, intrigued as he was in the pioneer scientist's insistence that created light and uncreated Light constituted one continuum. Interfaith monotheistic theology had affirmed this analogical truth for millennia. Torrance had not yet won the Templeton Prize or ventured into the remarkable set of books that included *Divine and Contingent Order*, *The Christian Frame of Mind*, and *Reality and Scientific Theology*. I have reviewed his work in *An Abrahamic Theology for Science*,[1] one volume in the interfaith series I have prepared for my classes over the last 20 years.

Ten years after Maxwell's incisive formulae were presented, Einstein followed with his earth-shaking summarial work of quantum theory and general relativity. Then, in the spring of 1921, he reluctantly came to the U.S. and was greeted as a rock star. This naïve puritan society so enamored with hope—especially Miltonian exuberance in science and technology and an all-too-readiness for eschatological war—saw only paradise regained in this frock of snowy hair. Both his Nobel prizes and his studies on relativity built on the data of light emissions received during an eclipse. This seemed to confirm, in that blessed mind beneath the hoary, frosty mane, that both darkness and light together were a divine emanation—at least in Spinoza's sense of world-spirit. To this well-prepared sight/light receptive mind, the sun's gravitational field bent a light beam, and light—far from being objectively constant—was amenable, vulnerable, and relative to the natural forces of energy and mass, to say nothing of supernatural forces. I recall one of the junior-high, rosy-cheeked cherubs asking Torrance about the sun standing still for Joshua. And I'll never forget his amazement at the answer. Something like, "What scripture always says, 'what is seen—is.'" By now, that kid must be a Calvinist theologian.

Beyond our sensible imagination, our moral imagination may wonder if Einstein also shared the mystic-moral *scientia* and *conscientia* of Arno Mayer, when in horror he asked, "Why did the heavens not darken?"[2] Was the 1917 eclipse also an "eclipse of God" (Buber) because of the horrific inhumanity of the First World War and the initial rumblings of *Shoah* throughout Europe? Was it happenstance or providence, I ask, that he and Eddington—two peace-lovers—were given the illuminating grace to see the form and substance of divine light manifest within mate-

---

1. See Kenneth L. Vaux, *An Abrahamic Theology for Science* (Eugene, Ore.: Wipf & Stock Publishers, 2007).

2. See Arno J. Mayer, *Why Did the Heavens Not Darken? The 'Final Solution' in History* (Princeton: Princeton University Press, 1988).

rial nature? But as we recall Hiroshima and contemplate the destructive capacity of explosive and radiative light, had perhaps the God of infinite mercy, love, and forgiveness (Exod 34:6) indeed turned his face, and had the light gone out even as the terror of a "thousand suns" (the *Vedas*) readied to irradiate the universe? Remember that it was two other pacifists—Weizsäcker and Oppenheimer—who gave us the bomb.

Sounding such an uncertain theological and cosmological trumpet, the *New York Times* greeted Einstein's disembarking in Port New York with these headlines:

- Lights all askew in the heavens;
- Men of science more or less agog over results of eclipse observations;
- Einstein's theory triumphs;
- Stars not where they seemed or were calculated to be; and
- But nobody need worry.[3]

GOD AS LIGHT

Our discussion of the theology of light must start against this historical and ethical backdrop, as we seek to connect these two variables: God and Light. The question is short and crisp. How, if at all, are God and Light connected, in any other sense than that of metaphor? First, a few musings from one of Jacob Neusner's 1000 books—this one on God.[4] In this interfaith study, he conjectures that just as Buddhism mysteriously arises from Hinduism, Christianity from Judaism, and Islam from Christianity—with the originating light generating, illuminating, and elaborating God (truth, light, word, good, beauty) while never diminishing the origination—so light (primal Torah) radiates into the world via Abraham, the Gentiles, and world faiths out into the remote crevices and edges of the cosmos. The history of God, therefore, is a history of light—one that will culminate in Neusner's words and Heschel's distillation of all four "Heavenly Torah

---

3. Walter Isaacson, "How Einstein Divided America's Jews," in *The Atlantic*, Dec. 2009.

4. Jacob Neusner, *God: Volume 1 of the Pilgrim Library of World Religions* (Cleveland: The Pilgrim Press, 1997).

traditions" (Biblical, Rabbinic, Kabbalic, and Hasidic) in the "redemption of humanity at the end of days."[5]

The "Peoples of the Book"—now three—formulate the conviction that God is light in two movements: sacred text itself and then in handmaiden religious philosophies. A religious philosophy arises in two movements: early Judaic and Christian philosophy and medieval interfaith philosophy. It is not yet certain whether the three movements of early modern Thomistic, Jewish, and Islamic philosophy will also assume similar formative cultural power to these classical and medieval syntheses.

By way of introduction to the issue, let us overview those developments in the history of God. The paper will then explore the formulation of a physical theology of light by Tom Torrance and a physiological ethic of sight as we glance at the work (science and ministry) of our own Kim Curnyn.

SACRED SCRIPTURE AND LIGHT

Images of light are profuse and diffuse in most ancient scriptures. Four thousand years ago, the traditions of the *Vedas* and Upanishads—what would become Hinduism and Buddhism and the Indo-European heritage—found the fundamental characteristic of human souls and the all-pervasive divine presence, *Nirguna Brahman* (the Nameless, Attributeless One), as having to do with light and enlightenment. The spiritual imprint of this primordial impulse is widespread and profound. When monotheism first arises in ancient Egypt and Persia, Africa and Eurasia, God as light and good is assumed. Hebrew consciousness in the faith of the wandering Arameans and Abraham sharpen this ancient and universal radiation into the *visio Dei* of interfaith monotheism—Judaism, Christianity, and Islam.

Rabbi Abraham Joshua Heschel was my first teacher of the blazing, yet gentle, light of the God of Abraham, Isaac, and Jacob—even in the midst of the dark cage of anguish our people have known throughout world history. Though I had pursued interfaith studies since my university time 50 years ago, and although my doctoral concentration in post-war Germany was in Holocaust studies and the abuse of science, technology, and medicine in the Third Reich, it was Heschel who taught me to honor my own Jewish heritage, to weep with him in Toronto when the wailing

---

5. Ibid., 1.

wall was reached in 1967, to anguish across the decades on the plight of the Palestinians, and to stand in spirit with him the night before his death—when he stood in the snow outside the Connecticut prison when Father Berrigan was released during the Vietnam War.

Heschel always taught us that God dwells in "deep darkness" (*arafes*)—which is His Light (I Kgs 8:12). With the priests on the Day of Atonement, we can only close our eyes at *Shekinah*, as the unutterable Name is uttered. Indeed, this project is the small gift of the presbyopic—old eyes—of your moderator, as he stands with you in awe before the Holy One who brought this faith heritage into being.

From the faith of the Hebrew people and from the rich tapestry of biblical Judaism, reflected in her sacred scripture, written and oral Torah, we select three central motifs that bear on light: 1) Universal light is the creature of God out of God's own disclosive (Torah-giving) nature; 2) The light of God and created light serve truth, justice, and love—the Way (Torah) of God; and 3) Light is the life and joy of humanity and of all creation. We explore these motifs in each of the three traditions.

Judaism

1. Sun, moon and stars, day and night is God's first creation. "Let there be light" is the first divine word and command. "And God made two great lights: the greater light to rule the day, and the lesser light to rule the night: he made the stars also" (Gen 1:16). God stakes his power and glory on his light. As in 2 Kings 11:36, where a son as successor to the King keeps his name from being extinguished, light is the perpetual seal of God's love for the creation—"while earth remaineth . . . day and night shall not cease" (Gen 8:22). Not to be confused with anything physical, as in pagan pantheism, God alone gives, takes, and ever mediates light—His creature.

2. Light is also moral disclosure. Job 24:14: "The murderer rising with the light killeth the poor and needy, and in the night is as a thief." In Hebrew scripture, the theme of wickedness going unpunished is addressed by the light of dawn that reveals the hidden malfeasance of the night. Torah is the lamp and lantern—the light to our way and lamp to our path. Light and illuminated

Way coalesce and cohere in God.

As I write at year's end, news comes of the death of Paul Samuelson. We all used his textbook in Economics I class. In one of his last interviews, he spoke of the dark labyrinth of gambling, bundling, deceiving, and risking the hard-earned investments, pensions, and savings of common people—by which investment bankers in the new cult of publicans we call the "finance sector" brought the world to the brink of economic collapse. More of the Keynesian than Friedman school, Samuelson said: "We were like Samson the blind. Monsters like me and my colleagues at MIT created instruments and mechanisms of spreading risk, not seeing what we were doing"—enriching ourselves while exploiting the poor (ABC Evening News, Dec 12, 2009). The crash of 2008 was brought to justice by the light of God, and the worms in the world's woodwork still scramble for darkness. Light and right are one in God.

3. Light is the fulfillment of Life. Psalm 139:11–12: "If I say surely the darkness shall cover me; even the night shall be light about me. Yea, the darkness hideth not from thee; but the night shineth as the day: the darkness and the light are both alike to thee." The ubiquity of divine presence penetrates within darkness and light. In the midst of dark, ominous, and threatening history, Esther and Mordecai lead the people in celebration of "light and gladness, joy and honour" (Esth 8:16). Biblical *shalom* means protection, peace, freedom, life, and light.

Christianity

1. Christian scripture finds its epicenter in the life-saving Gospel of Christ as the light of the world. "In Him was Life; and the Life was the light of humanity" (John 1:4). Rooted in the centuries-long yearning for Abraham's envisioned "offspring as the stars of the skies" (Gen 15:5) and Isaiah's servant Messiah who will be light to the Gentiles and establish Torah to the uttermost isles and glory to thy people Israel (Isa 42, etc.), the Jesus community finds the light of God in the promised Torah/Eschatology of Israel, which it finds further disclosed in Jesus as Messiah and Lord.

2. ". . . For God, who commanded the light to shine out of darkness,

hath shined in our hearts, to give the light of the knowledge of the glory of God in the face of Jesus Christ." The Apostle Paul formulates the essence of Christian enlightenment, in which the "god of this world" who has blinded the eyes, mind, and hearts of those who exist in idolatry, immortality, and injustice (Torah abrogation) is overcome by the glorious Gospel of Christ shining in the *imago Dei* of *Ebed Yahweh*—the divine servant. *En Christou* enlightenment of being now is part of, and in turn imparts, divine radiance into the world.

3. Christian scripture finally extols the doctrine of God's Light as reflected in human good works offered in the manner *Deus Illuminatio anima meum*. "Let your light so shine before men, that they may see your good works, and glorify your father which is in heaven" (Matt 5:16). Light ultimately derived from God is righteousness, displayed fully as human justice and love, pursuing the *telos* of world transformation *solo Dei gloriam*.

Islam

1. Sura 24 of the Qur'an, "An Nur" (light), summarizes Islamic scripture. Qur'an, which, like Torah and the law of Christ, is itself light, proceeds from Allah and shines into the homes of the *momineen* (believers). The precondition of receiving such light is purity, chastity, and fidelity to the law (*Taurut*). Human fidelity, justice, and veracity is reflected in and protected by public law (*Shariah*).

2. Through such personal, familial, and public devotion, *Taurut* guidelines proceeding from Allah Akbar illumine dark, hidden crevices of our lives and radiate from made-righteous lives out to the universe. Such guidance is given to every creature in the universe. "The book" is the supreme light for humans. For each faith community in the traditions of Abraham—Hebrew scripture, Christian scripture, Qur'an—is the particular receptacle, a tailor-made illumination fashioned by the One God of the world.

3. Divine guidance is like a candle (oil lamp) placed in a niche in the house where it illumines the whole room. Within a pure glass

(24:35), it radiates cleanly and compellingly to all. Through the light, Allah (Wahi) guides his people through the homes of the faithful and dutiful (24:36).

In this breviary of interfaith scriptural illumination, a range of issues is set before us. What does it say about whether we worship the same God? What does the phrase "Peoples of the Book" mean? Is that notion shared by the three faith traditions? What does such a conviction imply about reciprocal witness and proselytizing? Is it possible to formulate a new mode of cross-Abrahamic SR (Scriptural Reasoning) and Common Word mutual study—a kind of *midrash* that already seems to be taking hold among scripture scholars? The work of Kenneth Cragg, David Burrell, Jon Levenson, Aref Nayed, and others points in this direction. Project Interfaith explores these matters and will propose responses.

A PHILOSOPHICAL HANDMAIDEN FOR THEOLOGY

The harmony and synergy we find suggested among the three interfaith scriptural traditions is strengthened by two movements of concordance between philosophy, theology, and scripture. The first synthetic endeavor comes among Jews and Christians (and a diffuse phenomenon called Jewish Christianity) with Neo-Platonic philosophy. This liaison occurred in the first three centuries of the Christian era. The second profound interfaith movement occurs in the early middle ages—epitomized in *Al Andalus*—Moorish southern Spain—symbolized by the names of *Ibn Sina* (Avicenna), *Moshe ben Maimon* (Maimonides), and Padre Thomas of Aquino (Thomas Aquinas). The importance of these two moments in intellectual history for modern interfaith movements—which begin in the epoch of the Israeli/Palestinian conflict, the events of September 11th, and the war on terrorism and continue to this day—is inestimable. These philosophical concomitants to the monotheistic theologies—with a declared synergy of revelation and reason—will firmly imbed a theology of light into Abrahamic theologies and into a nascent interfaith theology and into world sacred history.

"THE CLASSICAL SCHEME"

What is called the "classical scheme" involves the Neo-Platonic harmony of Aristotle and Plato into books I and II of the *Enneads* of Plotinus, erroneously labeled the "Theology of Aristotle." This work takes steps toward the scriptural assertion of God as Creator, by speaking of emanations of the One who is in transition from Plato's *Demiurgos* to the radical and free creator of Genesis. The sublime being that Plato envisioned as illuminating the cave of human consciousness is associated with the One who said "Let there be light." What wins the day with Judaists like Philo, Hillel, and Gamaliel and Proto-Christians like Paul the Apostle, shadowy figures like Dionysius the Areopagate, and the magnificent train of first Christian theologians: Clement of Rome, Polycarp of Smyrna, and Irenaeus of Lyon, is the biblical God—the maker of heaven and earth. David Burrell summarizes, in a section entitled "External Creator of Contingent Reality" in *Knowing the Unknowable God*, his view equating Plato's first principle of the reality of God with light: "Platonism is an intellectual mysticism whereby we can ascend to a fine point of unified light which lies beyond articulation."[6] God in biblical purview is not Neo-Platonic emanation, but that wisdom has helped form the receptive atmosphere of transcendent monotheism as it will comprehend the God of Israel, Jesus, and Mohammad.

The incipient monotheism in Plato and the idealists and Aristotle and the naturalists, along with the ethical monolatry of Socrates and the Stoics, comes to the fore as a rational framework is joined to the revelatory impulse, and light breaks forth. As nature is linked with spirit in the profound wisdom begun with Pythagoras, realms of the created and the uncreated are conjoined in the sovereignty of the God of Abraham and Israel, the Father of Jesus the Christ, and Allah of Muhammad. The structure of the cosmos is intertwined with the world of angels and divine spirit, all accessible within the theory of human knowledge and action. Logos, angels, and light shine upon the persons who had walked in darkness, and great light glistens throughout the dark night of the Roman Empire's lethal assault on Jews and Christians.

This concordat of theology and philosophy will characterize Judaism and Christianity forward into the rise of Islam and on into the late middle ages, where it will be corroborated by another development.

Before we move to that point, let us digress to comment on the theological significance of this enlightening confluence. Since at this moment in history, we are only talking about the Jewish and Christian revelation,

---

6. David B. Burrell, *Knowing the Unknowable God: Ibn-Sina, Maimonides, and Aquinas* (Notre Dame, Ind.: University of Notre Dame Press, 1992), 92.

let us ponder the miracle/parables of Hanukkah and messianic healing, both believed to be manifestations of light.

HANAKKAH AND MIRACLE

Hanukkah is an historical parable in which the notorious Hellenistic Syrian King—Antiochus IV—violated the Jewish temple with his own idolatry until it was liberated by Judah, the Maccabee, in 165 b.c.e. The temple was reinstated and the Menorah rekindled. Oil of pure olive was present—sufficient for one day. As the eight-day vigil unfolded, refreshing supply miraculously appeared. This became the basis of the Festival of Lights—Hanukkah. As with the loaves and fishes, the miracle could be supernatural or natural, i.e., the generosity of those who had secreted a supply under their coats—no matter, same miracle.

The theological point of the miracle/parable is of profound gravity. A suppressing power had arisen over the Jewish people that sought to suppress their faith and would—through the Roman occupation—seek to eliminate their presence in the world.[7] A tyrannical power sought to extinguish the scripture, the people, and the presence of their God in the world. They sought—as history would bear out in Roman Reich I, II, and III—to exterminate that presence and light from the world. This makes the biblical-philosophical concordat of that historical epoch a decisive matter on earth and in heaven.

A similar Christian miracle/parable has the same import. Rodney Stark, in *The Rise of Christianity*, extols the new way of belief and life that Judaic and Christic culture transforms ancient pagan and Graeco-Roman culture.[8] Faithfulness replaces idolatry; esteem and protection of life replaces abortion, sex-selective infanticide, and pederasty. Fidelity in marriage and family life replaces promiscuity; the sick and dying are companioned not abandoned; justice and peace replaces contempt for the poor and violence toward others. The deep parable—derived from Egypt through Israel—extols a miracle where the lame walk, the sick are healed, the blind see, the poor hear good news, and the dead are raised. The gospel, which is light, conveys this light into the world. "What do you

---

7. See Martin Goodman, *Rome and Jerusalem: The Clash of Ancient Civilizations* (New York: Knopf, 2007).

8. See Rodney Stark, *The Rise of Christianity: A Sociologist Reconsiders History* (Princeton: Princeton University Press, 1996).

see? asks this Torah/Gospel Way." The answer: "The blind see . . ." and blessed are those who find no offense and are given eyes to see—Einstein and Eddington. "The people who dwelt in darkness—on them has light shined" (Isa 60:2).

THE MEDIEVAL CAMELOT

As we languish in the dawning 21st century after the events of September 11th, Afghanistan, Iran, Iraq, and Israel/Palestine and the seeming unending interfaith strife they symbolize, 13th-century Cordoba with Maimonides, Averröes, and a vital Catholic presence seems like an elusive medieval Camelot. The synthesis of theology and philosophy achieved here, reminiscent of the first Christian centuries, was indeed a continuation of the earlier consolidation. David Burrell, our keynote theologian in this project, puts it this way:

> This study of Ibn-Sina, Maimonides, and Aquinas intends to show how Muslim, Jew, and Christian conspired to fashion a doctrine of God by transforming classical philosophy to display divine transcendence.[9]

The rise of the three sibling Abrahamic faiths in history, accompanied by the *aggiornamento* with philosophy, led to a peculiar disposition toward natural and supernatural reality. Creating what has been called paradoxical hermeneutics, we now speak as follows:

- God is known and cannot be known.
- God is light and darkness.
- God is rational and irrational.

In sum, a *via Negativa* is discerned as a quality of Torah Way insisting in the spirit of the first three commandments—no other gods, no false idols, no contortion of the Name (*Hashem/Shemah*)—God cannot and must not be defined or confined. In our age of rampant infidelity, idolatry, and blasphemy along with fulminating injustice—transgression both within and without the realm of religion—the light of God is reflected and refracted, but also obscured within human thought and action.

David Burrell is thus guided in his call to interfaith faith and justice by the Vatican II teachings of Karl Rahner as he reflects about the church

---

9. Burrell, *Knowing the Unknowable God*, ix.

and, more broadly, the people of God in the world. Rahner reasons that there are three genuinely universal periods in the history of the church conceived as the household of God (ecumenical family): 1) the period of Jewish Christianity; 2) the period of Hellenistic, and then European, culture; and finally 3) "Today, when the church's life is the entire world." At this formative period of world-conscious faith, Karl Rahner would collaborate with Joseph Ratzinger on papers that related faith to this new world. In this thrilling new day of Vatican II, I remember meeting Rahner, with whom I was then studying along with Wolfhart Pannenberg, at a bus stop in Munich near the English Garden. Approaching 80 then, Rahner introduced me to his mother who was over 100—ah sweet, child-like faith!

But the potential interfaith age was soon beset by faith-based turmoil. Ratzinger, now Pope, circled the wagons—Vietnam, Muhammad Ali, and Dr. King's speech at Riverside Church, Rwanda, bombings in Sudan and Kenya, and then September 11th and the war on terrorism. Now it becomes Palestine and Iraq, Afghanistan and Iran. The sweet promise and interfaith prospect has succumbed to suspicion and a hardening of religious walls. A glimmer of hope and a dimly-burning wick now glows in Barack Obama at Detroit and Philadelphia, Cairo and Stockholm—as he offers a glimmer of hope despite the dark-dumpster always unloading on him.

Despite the challenges, we are still in an age fascinated by interfaith Scriptural Reasoning, "Common-Word" exercises and dialogues, and countless interfaith service projects. In this time of cautious exuberance, the church is involved in radical ecumenicity and in major "back and fill" endeavors with Judaism and Islam. A new missiology may be arising. As Catholicism seeks to become a "world religion," it revisits associations with the Eastern churches, Protestantism, Pentecostalism, and Evangelicalism—as well as with Judaism, Islam, and the religions of India and China—even atheistic humanism. As Rahner, Schillebeeckx, Congar, de Lubac, Lonergan, and others guide Vatican II, the church's quest for "perfect love of God and neighbor" is echoed by the same call from global Islam ("A Common Word").[10]

An analogy, again from the science of light, may pertain to the "dimly flickering wick" of interfaith endeavor. When Einstein and Eddington—

10. Karl Rahner, "Towards a Fundamental Interpretation of Vatican II," *Theological Studies*, 40, no.4, 1979, 716–27.

the Jew and Quaker, both men of peace—saw the light, it was precipitated by the corroborative evidence of three forces: 1) the wobbly ellipses of Mercury around the sun (the "topsy-turveyness [relativity, indeterminancy] of the world"); 2) the gravitational bend in the vector of light (a seeming infarction in the perfect beam); and 3) quantum theory (where light was found in all particular minutiae of the world). A delicate tapestry of an exquisitely colored interfaith fabric may be similarly arising today from the tattered fibers of religious strife.

TORRANCE AND THE THEOLOGY OF LIGHT

With the background of these preliminaries, we can now offer a set of persuasions on our subject with reference to the work of Torrance on the theology of light. Torrance achieved the Templeton Prize for contributions to the science/theology interface. He offers the concept that science has been transformed by theology in recent times, and that science, in turn, has transformed theology—especially in doctrines of creation and redemption.

Torrance begins with physics. Taking the teaching of his Edinburgh city-neighbor, Clerk Maxwell, and his epochal set of formulas to describe electromagnetism, he affirms Maxwell's claims: 1) that created and uncreated light are cognate phenomenon; and 2) that sound, color, light, speech (word), and therefore truth and good, are interrelated. The second thesis begins with the notion that luminous and electromagnetic radiation are now embraced by one mathematical formula. What the scientific world calls "the Muslim science"—optics—is therefore part of the electromagnetic epistemology. This epistemological revolution is necessary because of what we can now know about the human mind and its correlation with the mind of God.

Torrance then offers a set of propositions on God and light. He begins by claiming that three characteristics of physical light illumine the question of the nature of God: constancy, invisibility, and inaudibility.

- *Constancy*. Perhaps the most fundamental constancy in the realm of nature is the speed of light. Light cannot be defined by any contingent reality beyond itself. Einstein discovered that the speed of light remained the same, irrespective of any motion on the part of the observer.[11] Torrance reasons—with Augustine

11. T. Torrance, "The Theology of Light," *Christian Theology and Scientific Culture* (Oxford, U,K.: Oxford University Press, 1981), 78.

and Aquinas—that constancy in the universe can only come from an ultimate source of constancy unconditioned by anything other than itself.[12] The same assertion about God and the world goes two ways: light is, and acts as it does, by virtue of God, and this character of light attests to God. Rather than being circular reasoning, we have here the reciprocal reasoning of the psalmist "The heavens witness the Glory (light) of God and the firmament shows God's handiwork" (Ps 19:1). The constancy of light is not only analogous to the faithfulness of God, but light takes on derivative meaning by virtue of the creation. Torrance also finds *Shemah/Hashem* honor and correlative iconoclasm, the doctrine of grace and creative word and command as rooted in the divine nature as illuminator of creation.

- *Invisibility*. The invisibility of light and the doctrine of the invisibility of God are also reciprocally suggestive. "The realization that we cannot see light itself but only things lit up by light and of the relevance of this fact for our knowledge of God"[13] has long been a tenet of belief in the faiths of Abrahamic tradition. The Scots' hymn is well known:

    > Immortal, Invisible God only wise,
    > In light inaccessible hid from our eyes,
    > Most blessed, most glorious the ancient of days,
    > Almighty, victorious thy great Name we praise.
    > Great father of glory, pure father of light, thine angels adore thee,
    > all veiling their sight
    > All laud we would render, o help us to see,
    > 'tis only the splendor of light hideth thee.[14]

    As the cosmologies of "dark-matter" and "black holes" are related to cosmic brilliance," so, in a strange way, physical light is at once a darkness in itself and yet the source of brightness all around it."[15] Similarly, in numerous mystical philosophies—such as that of

---

12. Ibid., 81.

13. Ibid., 87.

14. Walter C. Smith, "Immortal, Invisible God, Only Wise," lyrics (1876), after I Tim 1:17, Traditional Welsh Melody, music (1839), http://songsandhymns.org.

15. Torrance, "The Theology of Light," 89.

St. John of the Cross—darkness and shadow are *illuminatio Dei*. Rembrandt and Vermeer, as well as their *nachfolger* Vincent Van Gogh—the glorious pastor/painter of color and light, comprehend and act out this truth. Even in the cave of Plato's darkness and shadow, of Pastor Van Gogh's Belgian coal mines and the tangled turmoil of his mind, or in the dark beauty known to the blind, deaf, and mute—God's sight, sound, and speech—God's light—is ever-present.

- *Inaudibility*. The connection of sound and light also offers intrigue. The science of Simplicius in the fifth century, Father John Philoponos in the sixth, mediated to the West by Avicenna and Al Ghazali in the 11th, then taken up by Robert Grosseteste—who, with Scotus, Bacon, Ockham and the 13th-century Oxford Franciscans developed the cosmogony of light—became an interfaith metaphysics of light. This fascinating synthesis of mathematics, philosophy, and theology saw light as the fundamental matter of the universe—the underlying cause of all change, motion, and sound. Torrance summarizes: ". . . here, too, is a conception of creation as a universe of light held (in coherence and cosmos/Colossians) under the overarching principle that the eternal light of God is the light of all things by which their light is lighted."[16]

  But here, the razor that opens and mends also cuts. Created light is silent, mysterious, though inaudible. The uncreated light of God is most audible—profuse with *Logos*, speech, Word, and sound. For Torrance, God's Word and God's light co-inhere in one another, and it is, as such, that they are the creative Source of all intelligibility in the universe."[17]

  Here also the synergic mystery of science and theology is felt. If we were to fathom the cosmic history of Einstein's particles or photons, or were we to gaze out on the phenomenon of the birth and death of stars here in the observatory in the seminary's back yard, we would hear the sounds of the first creation as across millions of light years those sound/sight rays at long last greeted our eyes.

16. Ibid., 90.
17. Ibid., 99.

In summary, the first contribution of Project Interfaith is that of offering suggestive hints of new adventures in science, philosophy, and theology that appear in the interfaith lens. We offer our efforts in this consultation to the numerous institutions, programs, and projects that will now carry on this endeavor.

CURNYN AND THE ETHICS OF SIGHT

We now turn our attention to our second task, the practical, pastoral side of Project Interfaith.

A few short decades ago, a young medical scholar came to my office at the University of Illinois. In the tradition of William of Ockham, I was officed in the department of surgery, even though the only cutting I did was *Seelsorge* (soul-shaving). Kim Curnyn had been a religion major at Notre Dame, was completing her medical studies, and now embarked on a course of a Ph.D. in philosophy and residency in ophthalmology. We met again several times in an interfaith setting, when father Hesburgh invited a trio called the "unholy trinity" to lead alumnae ethics conferences for Notre Dame's thousands of physicians. Reb Mark Siegler, clinical ethics pioneer of the University of Chicago, was our physician *Father*; Jim Bresnahan, lawyer and theologian was Loyola and Northwestern's Jesuit *Son*, and I was the uncanny *Shavuot Spirit* –a protestant Pastor and University of Illinois ethicist. Kim and her dad, Arnold, have been colleagues in the interfaith quest across the light-years since.

One other experience from my three decades in the medical school and hospital is relevant to the light/sight matrix. I tried to arrive before dawn at the University Medical Center, especially when I participated in medicine rounds with the house staff. I parked along Roosevelt road near Damen and walked the short block to my office and the hospital. In my role as university bioethicist, I would sometimes consult on patients at the West Side Veteran's Administration or Cook County hospital, but mostly rounded with the interns in internal medicine at the University hospital. Walking down the still dark street—an eerie feeling at first—became one of my greatest delights across the years. My path took me by the Lighthouse for the Blind and the other State-of-Illinois institutions serving the visually impaired. Each morning, I was greeted either by a slight woof by one or another seeing-Lab or more often "Ken, is that you?" We guided each other through the night street crossings and kibbutzed about the Chicago Bulls. These regular friends became my first guides and teachers to that awesome entourage of courageous saints—poor moms with their babies traipsing through the snow to the crowded public charity clinics—medical colleagues, nurses and family visitors keeping watch and vigil.[18]

THE BIOETHICS OF SIGHT

It was here that I first began to explore the range of ethical issues that orbit around the axis of sight. I learned that the positioning of human normality and normativity in seeing had visited a great injustice on the blind—persons who often saw worlds hidden from those with 20/20 vision. Kim and I would teach residents and consult attending on difficult cases. Surgical and oncological issues such as retinoblastoma presented moral quandaries—for example, removing encapsulated tumors also removed sight. Research on visual stimulation and virtual activation of sight through advanced technology and interventions in the optic centers of the brain proffered profound hope, but also presented the social justice anguish of availability and distribution.

Several matters of ophthalmologic ethics have also become acute in our world of contrived and caused differentiation of rich and poor. We take a holistic and systemic overview. River-blindness—a highly preventable and treatable devastation—afflicts millions. The absence of health care, home, work, education, and opportunity robs perhaps half the world of its birthright of vision and hope. Economic devastation and ecological calamity—of human making—only exacerbate the crisis, as the world becomes an apocalyptic nightmare. A realistic glance would agree with Reinhold Niebuhr, that God's good world is getting better and better and worse and worse at the same time.

On the bright side, cataract and *Prakash* clinics offer blessing as medical groups like Kim's bring sight to the blind and health to the sick. On the morally dark side, freedom of press sheds light on regimes where organs and tissues such as corneas are harvested from the dead and neo-mort prisoners without consent. On the light side, great city-of-hope vessels embark and land on the coasts of Africa, India, Bangladesh—not like

---

18. See elaborations in my autobiography, *Ministry on the Edge: Reflections of an Interfaith Pioneer, Civil Rights Advocate, and the First Bioethicist* (Eugene, Ore.: Wipf & Stock Publishers, Inc., 2010).

Tiger Wood's vessels of disgrace pursued by the multitudes of sensation-seeking media and paparazzi—but as unnoticed grace-givers, giving free medical care in the name of the "Light of the World," Red Cross, Red Crescent, Jewish charities—secular NGO's and international governmental aid.

Far and away, the most compelling issues of our theme concern sight for the blind. What are the physiological ethics of sight implicit in an interfaith perspective on human life in this God's good world? We begin with a review of Torah, Gospel, *Taurut* imperatives of bringing sight to the blind.

TORAH

Theophany and theotyphlosis (blindness or obstruction) are powerful images in Judaism. Theocentric etiology of blindness and impediment as gift is controversially presumed: "Who maketh the dumb or deaf, who gives sight or blindness. It is I, said the Lord." (Exod 4:11). More than the facile Deuteronomic equation of righteousness with health and illness with sin, we find more nuanced judgments. An inscrutable etiology and teleology occurs both within and from without this world—natural and supernatural—so much for Hippocrates, where even the sacred disease of epilepsy is of naturalistic derivation and therefore amenable to repair. Yet the God-story goes much deeper than blessing and punishment. Yahweh (Exod 3) and the Son of Man (Ezek 1:26) are actually One who sympathizes with human suffering—the advocate and purveyor of life and health—one who companions us through adversity.

Scriptural Reasoning on the burning-bush narrative has illumined this groundwork that Judaism provides to this interfaith *midrashic* chain. In Exodus 2 and 3, Yahweh has *seen* the oppression of his people, has *seen* Moses killing the Egyptian despite his hiding the body in the sand all after Moses had *seen* his victim killing an Israelite brother. After *hearing* the cries of the oppressed, God calls out of the burning bush, *shines* out in its burning (though it is not consumed), and says "I am the God of your Fathers—Abraham, Yitzak, and Yacov." A drama of light and sound, fire and Word plays out as a moral theophany. It is about oppression and a double murder.

All this constitutes a vision and call of God—for real. *Yahweh yireh* (God who sees and remembers) is disclosed as *ehyeh aser ehyeh*—God who is. Son of Man—*Ben Adam*—so like *Yahweh*—watching and walking gently and non-coercively with creatures in the world, is silently making it right and good again. This God is Firth's "ideal observer," much like Jesus weeping over a proleptic vision of a Jerusalem reduced to rubble—not intervening, but sharing the anguish. Being seen and seeing for good—identity and solidarity, human freedom and responsibility—are linked, therefore, in the reality of God. Enraptured in *visio Dei* and *vocatio Dei*—sight and call–for humankind, freedom, and duty is inescapable.

From this matrix of answer-ability (response—ability, *Verantwortung*)—"Adam, Cain, where are you?"—rises the imperative to give sight to the blind. In Christian tradition "I was blind, now I see" becomes faith's watchword. As in Hebrew scripture where taking bribes ("gifts") (Exod 23:8, Deut 16:19), blinds one to good and evil, in Christian vision, freedom releases one from the prison of ignorance and unseeing. Ignorant ministers and deceitful teachers are blind leading the blind—false shepherds. Hoodwinking is blinding and destroying—and lying, or what we euphemistically today call advertising—is a form of con or blasphemy.

The Shephardic task is for us to guide one another from self-distortion into truth and good –which is beauty. Politics, teaching, peacekeeping, business, advocacy, healing, ministry, parenting, neighboring, are all Shephardic vocations. The good shepherd guides to and safeguards the gate—she is the door and lies down to protect it from aggressors and transgressors. The sheep see her staff, hear her whistle and voice, then follow her leading.

The moving crescendo of sight-healings in the Gospels points toward this miracle of grace that is the essence of Abrahamic wisdom.

GOSPEL

> Brightest and best of the stars of the morning, Dawn on our darkness and lend us thine aid; Star of the East, the horizon adorning, Guide where our infant redeemer is laid.
> Vainly we offer each ample oblation, vainly with gifts would His favor secure;
> Richer by far is the heart's adoration, Dearer to God are the pray'rs of the poor.[19]

---

19. Reginald Heber, "Brightest and Best," lyrics (1811), http://www.hymnary.org.

Jesus spoke to conventional religious leaders then and now:

"You dishonor mother and father, by seeing their lives as a gift for your profit."
"You come near me with your mouth, but your heart is far from me." They are blind leaders of the blind—both will fall into the ditch (Matt 15).

Paul offers *midrash*:

We have renounced the hidden things of dishonesty—committing ourselves to everyone's conscience in the sight of God. We look not at the things which are seen, but at the things which are not seen—which are not temporary but eternal. (2 Cor 4)

Matthew continues:

When they objected that he healed sinners, republicans and the sick, Jesus said ". . . the well need no physician—but the sick" . . . and when he was in the house the blind came to him and he asked "do you believe I can do this?" They said "yes, Lord" and he touched their eyes and said, ". . . your faith heals you—tell no one." (Matt 9)

In Bethsaida, they brought a blind man to him and begged Him to touch him. He took him by the hand, led him outside of town; and when he had spit on his eyes and put his hands upon him, He asked him if he saw anything. "I see men as trees walking." He put his hands again on his eyes and made him look up—and he saw everything clearly (Mark 8).

. . . coming to Jericho, amid a great crowd, blind Bartimaeus sat by the highway, begging. When he heard the whispers that it was Jesus, he cried out "Jesus, you son of David, have mercy on me." The crowd told him to be quiet, but he cried out more loudly "you, son of David, have mercy on me." Jesus stopped. He stood still. "Bring him to me." The crowd called Bartimaeus and said "take heart—he is calling you." He cast away his garments and came to Jesus. Jesus asked: "what can I do for you?" He answered "Lord, could I see?" Jesus said, "On your way, your faith has made you whole and well." And immediately he received his sight and followed Jesus in the way. (Mark 10)

But the *textus classicus* is John 9:

As he went along, he saw a man blind from birth. His disciples asked him, "Rabbi, who sinned, this man or his parents, that he was born blind?"

"Neither this man nor his parents sinned," said Jesus, "but this happened so that the work of God might be displayed in his life. As long as it is day, we must do the work of him who sent me. Night is coming, when no one can work. While I am in the world, I am the light of the world." Having said this, he spit on the ground, made some mud with the saliva, and put it on the man's eyes. "Go," he told him, "wash in the Pool of Siloam" (this word means sent). So the man went and washed, and came home seeing. His neighbors, and those who had formerly seen him begging asked, "Isn't this the same man who used to sit and beg?" Some claimed that he was. Others said, "No, he only looks like him." But he himself insisted, "I am the man." "How then were your eyes opened?" they demanded. He replied, "The man they call Jesus made some mud and put it on my eyes. He told me to go to Siloam and wash. So I went and washed, and then I could see."

"Where is this man?" they asked him. "I don't know," he said. They brought to the Pharisees the man who had been blind. Now the day on which Jesus had made the mud and opened the man's eyes was a Sabbath. Therefore the Pharisees also asked him how he had received his sight. "He put mud on my eyes," the man replied, "and I washed, and now I see." Some of the Pharisees said, "This man is not from God, for he does not keep the Sabbath." But others asked, "How can a sinner do such miraculous signs?" So they were divided. Finally they turned again to the blind man, "What have you to say about him? It was your eyes he opened." The man replied, "He is a prophet." The Jews still did not believe that he had been blind and had received his sight until they sent for the man's parents. "Is this your son?" they asked. "Is this the one you say was born blind? How is it that now he can see?" "We know he is our son," the parents answered, "and we know he was born blind. But how he can see now, or who opened his eyes, we don't know. Ask him. He is of age; he will speak for himself." His parents said this because they were afraid of the Jews, for already the Jews had decided that anyone who acknowledged that Jesus was the Christ would be put out of the synagogue. That was why his parents said, "He is of age; ask him." A second time they summoned the man who had been blind. "Give glory to God," they said. "We know this man is a sinner." He replied, "Whether he is a sinner or not, I don't know. One thing I do know. I was blind but now I see!" Then they asked him, "What did he do to you? How did he open your eyes?" He answered, "I have told you already, and you did not listen. Why do you want to hear it again? Do you want to become his disciples, too?" Then they hurled insults at him and said, "You are this fellow's disciple! We are disciples of Moses! We know that God spoke to Moses, but as for this fellow, we don't even know where he comes from." The man answered, "Now that is remarkable! You don't know where he comes from, yet he opened my eyes. We know that God does not listen to sinners. He listens to the godly man who does his will. Nobody has ever heard of opening the eyes of a man born blind. If this man were not from God, he could do nothing." To this they replied, "You were steeped in sin at birth; how dare you lecture us!" And they threw him out. Jesus heard that they had thrown him out, and when he found him, he said, "Do you believe in the Son of Man?" "Who is he, sir?" the man asked. "Tell me so that I may believe in him." Jesus said, "You have now seen him; in fact, he is the one speaking with you." Then the man said, "Lord, I believe," and he worshiped him. Jesus said, "For judgment I have come into this world, so that the blind will see and those who see will become blind." Some Pharisees who were with him heard him say this and asked, "What? Are we blind too?" Jesus said, "If you were blind, you would not be guilty of sin; but now that you claim you can see, your guilt remains."

COMMENT

PowerPoint, if ever there was. I remember hearing Scottish Shakespearean actor Alec McCowan reciting the Gospel of Mark in a London theatre 40 years ago. That gospel hinges on the narrative of blind Bartimaeus, a most compelling visage in sacred scripture. Many at the theatre had been admitted free at McCowan's insistence, including several women of the street who sobbed in the seats next to us in the gallery as he spoke the King James version by heart. They had never heard this story or seen this light. What can we make of this cascade of texts—this verbal, then visual, picture? It is an immediate (*euthus*) transport to another reality—to use Mark's favorite adverb— a reality strangely present within this one, one that has transformed this world.

Though such texts are deleted from Thomas Jefferson's New Testament and the Jesus Seminar finds no authentic *logion* here—they are starkly authentic and alarming—therefore reliable. They also point to the inner meaning of miracle, which is the spiritual meaning of light in Christian but also in pan-Abrahamic tradition. The narratives witness to the sympathetic, even suffering God of *Tanakh*, the Bible, and the Qur'an.

The great commentator on John's Gospel—certainly a central Christian text on light—is the Roman Catholic Fr. Raymond Brown. He calls the gospel miracles—not literal historical data but *signs*. In these Jesus *logion*—cryptic and shrouded in ambiguity ("why didn't you return thanks"—"don't tell anyone")—we have Jesus' own identification with the oppressed and anguished, as well as that of the evangelist. More centrally, we have a depiction of the God of Moses—Yahweh and Ben Adam, Son of Man—as One who hears the cry and gives his concern and solidarity to the suffering. God, Hildegard of Bingen's "living light"—*sees* through human suffering, blindness, even death, to eternal light, truth, and health. God mediates and companions us through to that greater eternal life. Faith translates that realm of new being into the here and now.

TAURUT

Please—here, I'm on shaky ground. Drs. Bachir and Sahloul, I beg your pardon. The best I can offer is a few idiosyncratic reflections.

First, Qur'an as recitation seems fashioned for the blind. It is aural and oral light. Like Torah, Qur'an is best comprehended when chanted. In the Noor Institute for Islamic Studies in South Africa, Muhammad Islah is one of many blind students. He has completely memorized the 600 pages of the Qur'an. Islam, remember, is largely concentrated in what Christian missiologists call the "10-40 window"—the latitude band in which 90 percent of the population is Muslim. Here also is the concentration of the poor and the blind of the world. These are mysteries to contemplate. Why does Islam appeal to the poor (or very rich hit men like Osama bin Laden or the lonely son of a wealthy Nigerian banker)? Why do the poor gravitate to Islam? Max Weber has some conjecture on this question in his *Gesammelte Werke* sections on economics. Weber was also fascinated by the prosperity-tropism of Judaism and Protestantism. Why do these branches of Abraham's faith family tend to become middle class and wealthy? The question is theologically profound, especially if Judaism's Yom Kippur Liturgy is correct that the messiah will appear among the lepers and the poor, and Christianity's declared "God's preferential option for the poor" stands.

The pivotal teaching of Islam on sight to the blind is found in Sura 24 (*Al Nur*/The Light). The first theme is the affirmation that God controls the night and day and "this should be a lesson for those who possess eyes" (24:44). This is straightforward biblical assertion, where the creator of night and day—God who is Light—also is the giver of sight and blindness—insight and darkness of mind and spirit. The Spirit (law or way) of God illumines (casts light on) or conceals all that is perceived or is to come into being. Fundamentally, this is true, irrespective of whether one is blind or has sight. Those who have eyes can be blind and the blind can see. The inner meaning of creation is disclosure or revelation or faith. Without this divine activation and human reception, there is no light. King Lear, while seeing, is blind to life and love. Only when his blindness is graced by love does he come to awareness.

The second teaching is that God is non-discriminating—no respecter of persons. "The blind is not to be blamed ... nor is the handicapped to be blamed" (24:61). If the above premise is valid, then affliction is not a punishment (or a blessing), but an occasion of being touched by God and therefore being preyed open to self and others. As Father Damien found on Molokai, his fellow lepers now became worthy to mediate the sacrament—to be priests.

Sura 24:40 summarizes this mystery that is judgment and grace: "Another allegory is that of being in total darkness in the midst of a violent ocean, with waves upon waves in addition to thick fog. Darkness upon darkness—if he looked at his own hand, he could barely see it. Whomever God deprives of light will have no light." And we may surmise from all three scriptures of the Peoples of the Book: to whom God gives light . . . receives living light, the light of life.

CHILDREN OF LIGHT AND DARKNESS

Though of divine origin, sustenance, and destination, light is also presumed to be a human possession and function. Monotheistic faiths—especially in their apocalyptic variants—join Persian, Hellenic, and Hindu traditions in juxtaposing children of Light and Darkness in mimetic re-enactment of the transcendent struggle of Divine and demonic forces. Scriptural tradition demurs and rather concurs with Rabban Gamaliel: ". . . if (Light) is of God, it will prosper, if not, it will come to nothing" (Acts 5:34ff.). All biblical apocalyptic—Ezekiel, Daniel, Matthew 25,

Revelation—decalogically construe Light and Darkness. This Torah explication of Light is expressed in Paul's Epistle to the Ephesians:

> ... The eyes of your understanding being enlightened (Eph 1:18)

> ... though having been darkened, being alienated from the life of God (Eph 4:18)

> ... now put on the new man, created in righteousness and holiness (Eph 4:24)

> ... no anger, do not steal, lie, fornicate, covet, commit idolatry, utter vain words, uncleanness (Eph 5)

> ... rather forgive one another, walk in love ... now you are children of light ... walk in the light (Eph 5).

A real life parable makes the same point. Both belligerents thought of their own reprehensible actions as expressions of the light of justice and suppressions of the darkness of evil. In star-crossed rage, a *Hamas* rocket fired into Israel and an Israeli missile fired into Gaza left eight-year-olds Marya and Orel profoundly injured and near death. Now they find themselves mates in the same children's unit in the Jerusalem hospital hallowed by Chagall's Jerusalem windows. There, by the iridescent yellows and blues of Simeon and Levi, down the hall we hear Chagall's watchword warnings from Genesis: "... Weapons of violence are their swords" (49:5–6).

The young people are now inseparable, always in each other's rooms. Marya, a Palestinian Muslim with a severed spinal cord, and Orel, A Beersheba Jew with severe brain injury, are both children of Light—uncomprehending of the darkness of their respective politicians. As today they enjoy his mom's eggplant dish and her mom's rice and lamb, we can wonder with that primal physician and iconographer, Luke, whether the "children of darkness are wiser in their generation than the children of light ..." (Luke 16:8).

CONCLUSION

In his *Natural Theology* (1802), William Paley thought of strolling on the heath (perhaps where the great Hound of the Baskervilles then romped), where he came upon a stone and a watch. The first item, though wonderful, inspired no etiological mystery. But the second, how suggestive—like

Aquinas' causal proof of God—of the existence, yea, the necessity of a watchmaker. Much like the human eye, he conjectured, impossible without an exquisite design and construction. Charles Darwin moved in to Paley's rooms at Christ's College, Cambridge and shared the reverence as he pursued holy orders until that more compelling Ark bid his voyage. That latter-day voyager Richard Dawkins found not miracle but mistake in the blind watchmaker who had miswired "the eye in all vertebrates with the wires from each light-gathering unit sticking out on the side nearest the light and travelling over the surface of the retina where it passes through a hole the blind spot to join the optic nerve. Even the eyes in the Octopus and Squid were wired more rationally."[20] An Oxford lover of Gilbert and Sullivan should know that divine logic—so defiant of our little rules—often is "topsy-turvy."

Nevertheless, this essay celebrates Darwin and Dawkins, Einstein and Eddington, and even more, Mohammad, Moltmann, and Maimonides. Light is disclosed to inquiring and critical minds as well as to expectant and believing faith. As phenomenon, it is seen as material, metaphysical, and moral; arising in lineaments of influence and appropriation, it corroborates interfaith vision. Present in the ancient apperceptions we know from India and Greece, it radiates into the three monotheisms with vivid color—always greater than our narrow band of sight, more than we can ask or receive. Our hope is that dialogue at this workshop will be a spectroscope to glimpse that luminescence and color.

> God appears and God is Light
> To those poor Souls who dwell in Night,
> But does a Human Form display
> To those who dwell in Realms of Day.
>
> —William Blake

Kenneth Vaux, April 2010
Evanston, Illinois,
home of the 1954 Assembly of the World Council of Churches

---

20. Richard Dawkins, *The Blind Watchmaker: Why the Evidence of Evolution Reveals a Universe Without Design* (New York: W.W. Norton & Company, Inc., 1986), 93.

2

From Absolute Transcendence to Light
God's Ontological Generosity

Souleymane Bachir Diagne

MUSLIMS CONSIDER THAT IN chapter 112 of the Qur'an, known as "The purity of Faith," God introduced himself to the believers. In this surah, revealed in the early period of Muhammad's preaching in the city of Mecca, God answers the natural question raised by the people whom the declared prophet was calling to Islam about his nature, his quiddity. Here is that response: "Say: He is God, One. God, the Absolute. He begetteth not, nor is He begotten; and there is none like unto Him." The first remark is about the slight changes I have made in Yusuf Ali's translation. The first change is that I translate "Allah" as "God" because that is what the word means: nobody keeps *Gott* instead of saying "God" when they translate from German a sentence containing that word. The second, more substantive change is that I have kept one word "absolute" for the one corresponding word in the Quranic text, which is *samad*. The reason why Yusuf Ali preferred to be somehow redundant by translating "the Eternal, Absolute" (he does the same thing when he translates "the One and Only" for the word "One") is that *samad* is difficult to translate by one word as he explains in a footnote, commenting that the concept *samad* conveys the correlated notions of absolute existence independent from everything, self subsistence, and eternity. It has been often emphasized that while all the other attributes of God are repeated many times in different Quranic verses, this occurrence of *samad* is the one and only time the word is mentioned in the Book. As if one obvious way for God to emphasize his absolute transcendence was to use the word that describes it only once.

Understandably, there are traditions declaring that this one chapter 112 has the spiritual weight of one third of the whole Qur'an. In fact, if revelation is the way by which God makes himself known to his creation, this one chapter should even be equivalent to the totality of the Book, or even be the first and last word of it.

But then, how could there be any meaning attached to words and phrases such as "creation," "revelation," or "making himself known"? How would *samad* come out of itself in a revelation in order to be known by something having some kind of being called "creation"? A *hadith qudsi* (that is a prophetic tradition in which God is supposed to speak directly although what he says is not part of the Qur'an) thus declares: "I was a hidden treasure and desired to be known so I created a creation to which I made Myself known."

Of course there is no sound or even known chain of transmission for this *hadith* as custodians of orthodoxy immediately shout when it is quoted. And of course Sufis are the ones who would often quote it, not because of the external marks of its veracity but because of its internal self evidence. So maybe the meaning it carries is the one that can be read in this Quranic verse: "I have only created *jinns* and humans, that they may serve Me." (51:56) Maimonides has rightly stated, citing the Bible, that "the Thora speaks the language of the children of Adam." Revelation is for the creation to know God and not for God to describe himself as he is in himself in the terms that only *he* would understand and use.

So again God introduces himself to the people that Muhammad was calling to Islam: "God is the Light of the heavens and the earth. The parable of His Light is as if there were a niche and within it a Lamp: The lamp enclosed in a glass; the glass as it were a brilliant star; lit from a blessed tree, an Olive, neither of the East nor of the west, whose oil is well-nigh luminous, though fire scarce touched it: Light upon Light! God does guide whom He will to His Light: God does set forth parables for men: and God does know all things." (24:35)

It is common to the three Abrahamic religions and maybe to almost all religions that they oppose light to darkness. Thus the Qur'an certainly echoes the Bible in verses such as: "God is the Protector of those who have faith: from the depths of darkness He will lead them into light. Of those who reject faith their friends are the false gods from light they will lead them into the depth of darkness. They will be companions of the Fire, to dwell in there forever." (2:257) (Example: "But the children of the kingdom shall be cast out into outer darkness: there shall be weeping and gnashing of teeth," Matt 8:12).

Still, there is something quite peculiar in this self-description which keeps extending the metaphor of light by introducing all the elements that constitute a man-made luminary. What this extended metaphor says here, in this second divine self-introduction, is the willingness of God to offer himself in a parable, to liken himself. It is that likening which introduces the multiplicity, the profusion of realities enumerated here as niche, glass, lamp, oil, olive tree, star . . . Explaining his own nature in so many words, that is making it understood through sensible analogies, expresses "the desire to be known by creation" (through it and by it) which is also an expression of love. French philosopher Henri Bergson (1859–1942) has written that "divine love is not something from God: it is God himself" adding that "its description is interminable because the thing to describe is ineffable."[1] We have indeed moved from *samad* of which nothing can be said to the interminable profusion of Light. Light is the name of God as emanation of being, as profusion of being, as ontological generosity. God as *nūr* is the unfolding of God as *samad*.

It is not surprising therefore that the language of Islamic Neo-Platonism has made so many references to this verse of light, that of Avicenna (981–1037), of Al-Ghazali (1058–1111) or of Al-Suhrawardī (1155–1191). The third one, in particular, has built his "Philosophy of Illumination" (*Kitāb Hikmat al-Ishrāq*)[2] as a theory of successive emanations of Lights from the Light of Lights. Why would Light come out of itself? Why would *samad* unfold into being? Because, says Shihāb ud-Dīn Suhrawardī, the Light of Lights is pure "generosity" (*jūd*), as it pertains to the essence of light that "it reveals itself to and emanates upon every receptive one": to be effusive. That is what makes the image of lights proceeding from lights the best possible representation of the emanation of the many out of the One, since the One is supposed to produce what exists, not out of any necessity or even any reason: if God is Light, the desire to be known is not something that happens to him, it is something that is him. And in his book, Suhrawardī does evoke the "master visionaries"

---

1. Bergson, H., *Oeuvres* (Paris: Presses universitaires de France, 1959), 1189.

2. John Walbridge and Hossein Ziai, English Translation, Notes, Commentary, and Introduction (Provo, Utah: Brigham Young University Press, 1999).

of Neo-Platonism as having believed "the Maker of the universe and the world of intellect to be light": "When freed from my body I beheld luminous spheres," he quotes Plato as saying.[3] (In fact, he is confusing Plotinus with Plato). And he establishes some continuity between that "Platonic" belief and the Quranic revelation that "God is the Light of the Heavens and the earth" or the prophetic prayers addressing God in this way: "O Light of Light! Thou wouldst be veiled without Thy creation and no light would behold Thy Light"; or this other way: "I ask Thee by the Light of Thy countenance, which fills the pillars of Thy throne."

So Suhrawardī's cosmology presents itself as an infinite process of emanation of Lights, a process originated by the Light of Lights out of its desire and passion for Its own essence. And as Lights proceed from that passion, they become many, with always the higher light having dominance over the lower light and the lower light beholding the higher and having desire and passion for it. At the beginning there is the relationship between the Light of Lights and the first emanated, called by Suhrawardī the Proximate Light. That relationship is thus described by Suhrawardī: "The Proximate Light beholds and is illuminated by the Light of Lights. It loves the Lights and itself, but its love for itself is dominated by its love for the Light of Lights."[4] Then the relationship is indefinitely reproduced all along the chain of emanation: ". . . a second light results from the Proximate Light, and from the second a third, and likewise a fourth and fifth, up to a great number."[5]

Two points are to be added here, in order to present more completely Suhrawardī's cosmology of Lights constructed from the encounter between Neo-Platonism and the Quranic assimilation of God to Light. The first point answers the question: in this procession of incorporeal lights where does corporeality and darkness come from? The mechanism of production of this reality that Suhrawardī calls "barrier" (*barzakh*) is that in its contemplation of the object of its passion, the Light of Lights, the Proximate Light measures the distance from it, it acknowledges "the night of its own essence when compared to the Light of Lights," an ac-

---

3. *The Book of Illumination*, op. cit., Part Two, §171, 110.

4. Suhrawardī, *op. cit.*, Section 7; §148, 98. The Sufi notion of the cosmic nature of love can be founded on this relationship of dominance and love. Or, in the words of Henri Bergson: "God is love, and He is an object of love: the whole contribution of the mystic is there." (*Oeuvres,* 1189).

5. Ibid., Section 9, §148, 99.

knowledgement wherefrom a shadow is produced, which is the supreme *barzakh*.⁶

The second point is that the cosmos thus produced is infinite, because it has no reason to be finite. Before Giordano Bruno who was burned at the stake in 1600 for having uttered such a thesis considered then blasphemy, Suhrawardī held the view that it goes against the principle of sufficient reason to affirm that the results of the process of emanation should stop after ten (corresponding to Aristotelian cosmology) or even "a great number."

At the beginning of the third chapter of his main work, *The Reconstruction of Religious Thought in Islam*, Muhammad Iqbal (d.1938) compares the same Quranic verses, those of chap. 112 and the verse of light. He states that the verses of chapter 112 present God as the Ultimate Ego, "the perfect individual, closed off as an ego, peerless and unique [that] cannot be conceived as harbouring its own enemy at home."⁷ (Because, as Bergson, whom he quotes, said, only is an accomplished individual the being in which the tendency towards individuation does not cohabit with the antagonistic tendency towards reproduction). Concerning the verse of light, Iqbal opposes the view of Lewis Richard Farnell (1859–1934) who, in his Gifford lectures on the attributes of God⁸, read it as "an escape from the individualistic conception of God" and, indeed, as pantheistic. Iqbal's response is twofold. First, he states that "the development of the metaphor is meant rather to exclude the suggestion of a formless cosmic element by centralizing the light in a flame which is further individualized by its encasement in a glass likened unto a well-defined star."⁹ In other words, likening God with Light, the way the three Abrahamic religions do, is not to diffuse and disperse the essence of the divine but, on the contrary, to concentrate it, beyond the niche, beyond the lamp, etc., into one ultimate individual Ego. Second, Iqbal uses modern science and the fact that relativity has taught us the absolute nature of the velocity of light to claim that Light is therefore synonymous with Absolute. In the terms of our discussion, *nūr* is no other than *samad*.

6. Ibid., Book II, Section 4, §142, 98.

7. M. Iqbal, *The Reconstruction of Religious Thought in Islam* (Dubai, Kitab al-Islamiyyah), 62–63.

8. The lectures, delivered in 1924–1925, were published in 1925 by Oxford University.

9. Iqbal, *op. cit.*, 63.

Of course a modern individual, for whom the notion of the velocity of light being an absolute makes sense, could share in that reading. And why not make that modern notion part of the understanding of the verse of light, since one should always understand the sacred text in the present, from the perspective in which they are situated? How could one do otherwise anyway?

In fact, it is consistent with Iqbal's philosophy of a constant affirmation of the individual that he would insist on avoiding any interpretation that seems to dissipate the force of individuation and replace it by some cosmic sense of totality or infinity. But he does not need to add this strange scientific point to his first response to Farnell: that the verse of light is about individuality does not necessarily mean that it is about the Absolute in the sense of the absolutely not- relational. On the contrary, the understanding that the verse, in the end, speaks of the individual human ego in *relation to* the Ultimate Ego is valid and does go against that assimilation. The cosmological meaning itself, like the one developed in Suhrawardī's ontology of lights, sets the stage for this relation between the human ego and the divine One.

Because we are living lights ourselves, our human destination is the return to the Light of Lights. So the prayer in the Qur'an that says, (66:8) "Our Lord! Perfect our Light for us, and grant us forgiveness; for Thou hast power over all things," can be commented as meaning: "Our Lord, perfect us as the lights *that we are* by dissipating the darkness that we carry, for the power of illumination is all yours. . ." In any case it is important to note that "light" is a name we share with God, which establishes a bridge between us and the divine source.

That bridge can be considered to be the Prophet of Islam, as one of his name in the Qur'an describes him as the "light giving lamp" (*sirāj al munīr*). This description in turn may be connected with the well known *hadith* in which Muhammad declared: "I was a Prophet while Adam was still between water and clay." The Sufis in particular have often interpreted this prophetic saying as meaning that the prophetic reality (*haqiqa muhammadiyya*) or the prophetic light preceded existence created for its sake. Hence the spirit of the prophet or his "transcendent luminescence" "is itself the *barzakh* (isthmus) between the material world and that of the unseen ... between the material and spiritual natures of the human being."¹⁰

Abu Hamid Al-Ghazālī (d.1111) the well known theologian and Sufi has such an understanding of the verse of light which is both about individuality and relationality. In his work, *The Niche of Lights*, which is a commentary of the verse, he reads it as referring to the faculties of the human individual. Thus the human sensible spirit which receives information through the five senses is symbolized by the niche and its holes; the imaginal spirit (the Aristotelian *phantasia*) which retains images of the sensory data corresponds to the glass; the specifically human rational spirit is represented by the lamp; the faculty that resembles most a tree and its branches is the reflective one that produces thoughts not limited by space (east or west); it is an olive tree because its oil is used to enlighten and that oil symbolizes the prophetic spirit which is in all human beings. And because, the *telos* of the individual thus conceived, his or her nature is light, it is always ready to become what it has to be, "though fire scarce touches it" in which case it is as if light is making its connection with its own nature: light upon light.

It is interesting to make the remark that such a commentary by Al-Ghazālī perfectly echoes one made by Avicenna, of the same verse of light, in his *Kitāb al-'ishārāt wal tanbīhāt* (Book of Directives and Remarks). Avicenna comments the verse in the chapter devoted to "the human soul" and considers then that the metaphor describes the different human faculties. First, he says, there is a faculty which prepares the individual to turn towards the intelligible and which is therefore called "material intelligence"; that material intelligence is the niche. Then there is a faculty that is produced in the soul when the first intelligible principles are actualized in it; that faculty (which is the first one but perfected and close to being actual) is the *habitus* intelligence and is represented by the glass. Through it the soul is prepared to receive acquired knowledge, either by reflection (that is the olive tree) when it is weak, or by intellectual intuition (that is with the oil in addition) when intuition is stronger than reflection. So in the end the noble, matured faculty which is thus created is a holy faculty "whose oil is well-nigh luminous, though fire scarce touched it."¹¹

10. Zachary Valentine Wright, *On the Path of the Prophet. Shaykh Ahmad Tijani and the Tariqa Muhammadiyya* (Atlanta: The African-American Islamic Institute, 2005), 129–130.

11. Ibn Sina, *Le Livre des directives et remarques*, French translation by Goichon, Beyrouth (Paris: Vrin, 1951), 324–325.

There are two main reasons why it is important to emphasize the analogy of the two commentaries. The first one is to insist on the importance of the metaphor of light for Islamic thought, in particular Neo-Platonic cosmology and theory of knowledge. The second one to show that Al-Ghazālī, for all his strong opposition to the philosophers whom he accused of heresy is, in the end, one of them, as Averröes will say (in his *Decisive Treatise*) relativizing the theologian's anathema against philosophy.

CONCLUSION: TWO ASPECTS IN THE METAPHOR OF LIGHT

I will conclude by just reemphasizing two aspects of the theology of Light as developed from the Quranic divine name of *nūr*.

1. Monism is one aspect: it must be understood that likening God to Light does not amount to dualism or Manichaeism; there is not a principle of darkness to be opposed to the divine light; darkness, in other words, is not a being but sheer lack as the cosmology of Suhrawardī shows.

2. Individuality is another important aspect. That the Verse of Light has nothing pantheistic ultimately means that it is not a description of God (the Qur'an insists that he is beyond any description) but a description of the human being and an invitation for her to undertake the journey towards the light, to see it, and to become it.[12] Because the sight of light is the same as becoming the light that we are.

Souleymane Bachir Diagne
Presented at Garrett-Evangelical Theological Seminary
April 30, 2010

---

12. In the *Niche of Lights* Ghazāli establishes such a link between the cosmology of light and the Night Journey (*mi'raj*) of the human spirit modeled after the Prophet's *mi'raj*.

3

Light and New Creation in Genesis and the Gospel of John

K. K. Yeo

LIGHT AND NEW CREATION are interrelated concepts in Genesis 1–3 and in the Gospel of John (as well as in Isaiah and the Pauline texts).[1] This paper first explores the motif of pre-creation/ creation in Genesis and John, then examines how these two books use the clustered concepts of light, word, and life to advance their theologico-ethical purposes. Finally, the paper draws on insights from Genesis and John to propose three brief biblical principles for the construction of an enlightening and life-giving interfaith project today.

PRE-CREATION AND NEW CREATION THROUGH THE PRE-EXISTENT LOGOS-LIGHT

The biblical usage of light as a cosmic metaphor has strong theologico-ethical nuances, a metaphor that has universal appeal in its rhetorical per-

---

1. See Isaiah 32:14–18, 41:18–19, 55:12–13, 58:1–14, 65:17–25, 66:22–23; 2 Cor 5:17; Gal 6:15; Rom 8:18–22. Bernhard W. Anderson, *From Creation to New Creation: Old Testament Perspectives* (Minneapolis: Fortress, 1994); Richard Hays, *The Moral Vision of the New Testament Theology: Community, Cross, New Creation, A Contemporary Introduction to New Testament Ethics* (San Francisco: HarperSanFrancisco; 1996); Douglas J. Moo, "Creation and New Creation," paper presented at the Annual Meeting of the Institute of Biblical Research, Boston, MA, November 22, 2008; Moyer V. Hubbard, *New Creation in Paul's Letters and Thought* (Cambridge: Cambridge University Press, 2002); W. Hulitt Gloer, *An Exegetical and Theological Study of Paul's Understanding of New Creation and Reconciliation in 2 Cor. 5:14–21* (Mellen Biblical Press Series 42; Lewiston, NY: Mellen, 1996).

suasion and eloquence. The phenomenon of light is universal; similarly, theology and ethics are basic pursuits of all humanity.

Both the Genesis and the John texts begin with the phrase "in the beginning," *archē* (Ἐν ἀρχῇ, Gen 1a; John 1:1), which can mean an "era before time" or "the first cause." The pre-creation "era"/"aeon" (αἰῶνα, Matt 12:32; John 4:14; Heb 1:2) existed in "no-time" and "no-space" before created light existed. Since the pre-creation "era" existed in the realm of uncreated Light, this "aeon" often is associated with eternity, an era that exists forever, both before creation and apocalyptically.[2]

All four canonical Gospels, the Pauline Epistles, and the Apocalypse of the New Testament are re-readings of the Hebrew scripture,[3] which attempt to move from the theme of old creation to new creation (and varying only in degrees of intertextuality). None of these achieve this more effectively than the Gospel of John, whose new-creation motif can be seen in four distinct narrative schemes.

A. The preexistence of *Logos* as the Hebraic wisdom (*hokmah*) and the Hellenistic *logos* (including the cultural meanings of both concepts) embody the creative power of word/language/speaking, exemplified well in the creation theology of Genesis 1. But more than creative and rhetorical *Logos*, Johannine *Logos* amplifies its (en)light(ening)[4] and life(giving) power by creating the *telos* of superabundance (*zōēn aiōnion*, "eternal

---

[2]. Before the emergence of apocalyptic thinking though, the biblical narrative is concerned with living "in time" in God's created world because of God's light (uncreated and created) in the world.

[3]. According to Wolfgang Roth, in the Gospel of John, John the Baptist's testimony and the gathering of the first *five* disciples (1:19–4:54) form the first part of the canon (Prophets), followed by the second through the sixth sections of the Law (Deut, Num, Lev, Exod, Gen). See Wolfgang Roth, "To Invert or Not to Invert: The Pharisaic Canon in the Gospels," in *Early Christian Interpretation of the Scriptures of Israel: Investigations and Proposals* (ed. Craig A. Evans and James A. Sanders; Sheffield, U.K.: Sheffield Academic Press, 1997), 63–67; John Painter, "Earth Made Whole: John's Rereading of Genesis," in *Word, Theology, and Community in John* (ed. John Painter, R. Alan Culpepper, and Fernando F. Segovia; St. Louis, Mo.: Chalice Press, 2002), 65–84.

[4]. The term light (*phōs*) occurs 23 times in John 1:4, 5, 7, 8, 9; 3:19, 20, 21; 5:35; 8:12; 9:5; 11:9, 10; 12:35, 36, 46. To give light or enlighten (*phōtizō*) in 1:9.

life"[5]) for humanity through Christ the Light.[6] Consistent with the *topos* of "transformation to life" in the Genesis 1 narrative, John speaks of "believing"/"trusting"[7] as the receptive state of being necessary for eternal life: "But these are written so that you may come to believe that Jesus is the Messiah, the Son of God, and that through believing you may have life in his name" (20:31). It is telling that, while Genesis 1:1 has "in the beginning *God*," John 1:1 has "in the beginning *Logos*" (*Logos* here refers to the pre-existent Christ). The *Logos* was not only *with* God (John 1:1); the *Logos was* God (John 1:2).

B. Jesus' earthly ministry is narrated in a seven-day progression in the Book of Signs (*semeia*) that ultimately leads to the eighth day of the new creation, the eschatological day that signifies the work of salvation culminated on the cross (Lamb of God).[8] The first week and the last week of Jesus' ministry correspond to the first creation in Genesis 1 and can be represented as follows:[9]

---

5. The term "eternal life" (*zōēn aiōnion*) occurs 17 times in John 3:15, 16, 3:36, 4:14, 36, 5:24, 39, 6:27, 40, 47, 54, 68, 10:28, 12:25, 50, 17:2, 3. "Life" (*zōe*) occurs 36 times in John 1:4, 3:5, 16, 36, 4:14, 36, 5:24, 26, 29, 39, 40, 6:27, 33, 35, 40, 47, 48, 53, 54, 63, 68, 8:12, 10:10, 28, 11:25, 12:25, 50, 14:6, 17:2, 2, 20:31. On "light of life" (John 8:12), see also Job 3:20; 33:30; Ps 49:19; 56:13; Isa 53:11.

6. The Gospel of John speaks of Christ as light (1:4–5, 7-9; 3:19–21; 5:35; 8:12; 9:5; 11:9–10; 12:35–36, 46) and John the Baptist as a lamp (5:35).

7. The noun "faith" (*pistis*) does not occur in John, but the verb "to believe" (*pisteuō*) occurs 86 times in John: 1:7, 12, 51; 2:11, 22, 23, 24; 3:12, 15, 16, 18, 36; 4:21, 39, 41, 42, 48, 50, 53; 5:24, 38, 44, 46, 47; 6:29, 30, 35, 36, 40, 47, 64, 69; 7:5, 31, 38, 39, 48; 8:24, 30, 31, 45, 46; 9:18, 35, 36, 38; 10:25, 26, 37, 38, 42; 11:15, 25, 26, 27, 40, 42, 45, 48; 12:11, 36, 37, 38, 39, 42, 44, 46; 13:19; 14:1, 10, 11(2), 12, 29; 16:9, 27, 30, 31; 17:8, 20, 21; 19:35; 20:8, 25, 29, 31.

8. Andreas J. Köstenberger, *John* (Baker Exegetical Commentary on the New Testament; Grand Rapids: Baker Academic, 2004), 56.

9. Adaptation of a table in Andreas J. Köstenberger, *A Theology of John's Gospel and Letters: The Word, the Christ, the Son of God* (Grand Rapids: Zondervan, 2009), 349. See also D.A. Carson, *Gospel According to John* (Pillar New Testament Commentary; Grand Rapids: Wm. B. Eerdmans Publishing Co., 1990), 167–68; Thomas Barrosse, "The Seven Days of the New Creation in St. John's Gospel," *Catholic Biblical Quarterly* 21 (1958), 507–16.

First Creation in Genesis	First and Last Week of Jesus' Ministry in the Gospel of John		
Genesis	Word and sign pre-existed (John 1:1–51):	Word and sign to the world (John 2:1–12:50)	Word and sign to the faith community (John 13:1–21:25)
Creation through Speech-Light	Creation through Word-Light	Jesus' first week of ministry (John 1:29–2:11)	Garden (John 18:1; 18:26; 19:41; 20:15)
"In the beginning God..." (Gen 1:1)	"In the beginning was the Word..." (John 1:1–5)	The new birth into Kingdom of God (John 3:3; 3:5)	Jesus' resurrection on "first day of the week" (John 20:1–31)
The first creation (Gen 1–2)	The new birth as children of God (John 1:12–13)	Jesus Lord of the Sabbath (John 5:1–47; 9:1–41)	Creation of community (John 20:22)

In addition, repeated use of the phrase "the next day" in the Johannine narrative of Jesus' first week of ministry is intended to echo the sequence of the Genesis creation text:[10]

- Day 1: John's testimony regarding Jesus (1:19–28);
- Day 2: John's encounter with Jesus (1:29–34; "the next day");
- Day 3: John's referral of two disciples to Jesus (1:35–39; "the next day");
- Day 4: Andrew's introduction of his brother Peter to Jesus (1:40–42);
- Day 5: Philip and Nathanael follow Jesus (1:43–51; "the next day"); and
- Day 7: Wedding at Cana (2:1–11; "on the third day").

C. Roth argues rightly that the wedding at Cana is the "beginning" (*archē*) sign—the sign or symbol being the rhetorical genius of John in connecting the two worlds of above and below.[11] The narrative description of the six jars, representing six divine gifts Jesus brings to the broken

---

10. Köstenberger, *A Theology of John's Gospel and Letters*, 349.

11. Roth, "To Invert or Not to Invert," 64; R. A. Culpepper, *Anatomy of the Fourth Gospel: A Study in Literary Design* (Philadelphia: Fortress Press, 1989), 182–83.

creation, is reminiscent of the paradise lost in Genesis 2–3, but now regained in Jesus' works:

1. water of life / eternal water (Gen 2:6 and 10 / John 4:14);
2. bodily life / health instead of weakness (Gen 2:6 and 17 / John 4:14);
3. food for daily sustenance / heavenly manna (Gen 2:9 and 16 / John 6:32);
4. physical sight / spiritual discernment (Gen 2:9 and 3.6 / John 9:37–38);
5. life leading to death / death leading to life (Gen 2:17 and 3:19 / John 11:39–44); and
6. life giving breath / Holy Spirit (Gen 2:7 / John 20:22).

Roth relates the six gifts to the Johannine hermeneutic of inversion. He writes:

> The narrative strategy of inversion suggests that Jesus' mission undoes step by step, representatively and in inverse order, the gradual breakdown of the wholeness of God's creation as told in "the Law and the Prophets." The reversal is, as it were, a healing process in which the goal is complete restoration.... The story of the wedding at Cana (John 2:1–11) is the "master sign" because it is a parabolic preview of the Johannine work in its entirety: the water of "the Law and the Prophets," filled into six (!) jars, is transformed into the "wine" which Jesus' six gifts offer.[12]

D. In addition to the allusion to the garden of Eden in the wedding of Cana narrative, the Passion narrative is set first in the garden (*kepos*; 18:1; 18:26; 19:41). In the second garden scene (20:15–22), Mary identifies Jesus as the gardener (*kēpouros*; 22:15); although she is mistaken, it is possible that this is an ironic suggestion of Jesus as the new Adam/human[13] who has tended and mended the world (e.g., by being the golden serpent in 3:14; Num 21:9; cf. Gen 3:1–14). The risen Christ breathing the Spirit on his followers (20:22) is reminiscent of God breathing life into the "dusty" Adam (Gen 2:7; cf. also Ezek 37:9). Jesus' resurrection also is

---

12. Roth, "To Invert or Not to Invert," 66–67.
13. Pilate calls Jesus "the man" (*Ecce homo*, John 19:5), see also the following reference to Jesus as "the man" (John 5:11, 12, 13, 15; 7:25, 9:9, 11).

portrayed as the beginning of a new creation, i.e., "first day of the week" (20:1; 20:19; cf. 1:3) and the phrase "a week later" (20:26), as well as the narration that Jesus had completed his work (19:28; 19:30).[14] Earlier on, John's narrative recounts Jesus performing several signs/miracles (works) on the Sabbath (5:9b, 17; 9:3-4, 14). While God rested from all his works on the Sabbath (Gen 2:2), now Jesus, on the "eighth day," consummates God's work of eternal life for humanity.

That the Christocentric reading of created light coming from the uncreated Light, and how these two lights provide a synergy of creating the cosmos, is explicitly in John and later Christian tradition. We will concentrate below on how John uses the Genesis motifs to his advantage.

I. LIGHT AS PERSONIFIED WISDOM/LOGOS

Light in the Bible symbolizes the wisdom of God, a sensibility alert to the mystery of all things and guidance for all to live charitably and harmoniously within the *oikonomia* of God. From the Genesis text, God as Light and God's created light are analogies for God's wisdom, which made visible God's goodness in the world from the beginning.

It is this very wisdom (Light and light) that creates and inhabits the world. In John's language, the *Logos* "enfleshed and pitched his tabernacle among us" (1:14), and in Genesis' language, the Light sheds light on a world of void and darkness (1:1-2). It is this wisdom of God's utterance that initiates life, light, and meaning into the world. The power of God's *Logos* is to create: "so shall my word be that goes out from my mouth; it shall not return to me empty, but it shall accomplish that which I purpose, and succeed in the thing for which I sent it" (Isa 55:11).

According to Genesis 1, God created the world in "double exposures;" one by creating light through utterance/chanting of "let there *be* . . . light" (Gen 1:3), and the other by enlightening/appreciating the light with delight: "and God *saw* that the light was *good*" (Gen 1:4a). What a powerful, beautiful, and joyful lyric! God's light allows people to see and to understand. The wisdom of God is this joyful affirmation of the cre-

---

14. Derek Tidball, "Completing the Circle: The Resurrection according to John," *Expository Times* 30 (2006), 169-183. See also Jan A. DuRand, "The Creation Motif in the Fourth Gospel: Perspectives on Its Narratological Function within a Judaistic Background," in *Theology and Christology in the Fourth gospel: Essays by the Members of the SNTS Johannine Writing Seminar*, ed. G. van Belle, J.G. Van der Watt, and P. Maritz (Leuven: Leuven University Press, 2005), 21-46.

ative light, a light that offers perspective for understanding (or framing) of things already in existence but unclear in terms of worth or purpose in the greater scheme of life.

The coming of light allows God, who is Light, and human beings, the created image/"positive" of God, *to see* goodness as the worthiness and matrix of God's creation. It may seem paradoxical to speak of God as the Light whose perception of the created world is helped by the created light. But the point in Genesis 1:4a, even taking into account the limitations of language, is not about God's ability or inability to see (with or without light), but about God's *wisdom* in seeing the light he spoke into existence as good—that is, light in Genesis 1:4a is not simply physical light, but a metaphor for wisdom. Later Wisdom literature pays attention to the "eyes of God" in overseeing wisdom in the world: "For human ways are under the eyes of the Lord, and he examines all their paths" (Prov 5:21); "The eyes of the Lord are in every place, keeping watch on the evil and the good" (Prov 15:3); "The eyes of the Lord keep watch over knowledge, but he overthrows the words of the faithless" (Prov 22:12); and "The discerning person looks to wisdom, but the eyes of a fool to the ends of the earth" (Prov 17:24).[15]

Not surprisingly, John's use of sign (*semeion*) in 6:2, 14, and 26 is connected to the act of seeing; thus, signs and symbols grant readers a deeper vision of the greater reality.[16] Both the Judeo-Christian tradition and *Zhuangzi* uphold the vision of *shalom* (e.g., James' "faith and work" and "perfect person"), as human beings befriend Light and delight in each other. In the Chinese wisdom tradition, *Zhuangzi* articulates this clearly in saying that a "true person" (*zhengren*) and shaman (*wu*, i.e., the transcendental intermediary between the physical and spiritual worlds) is the one who befriends wisdom, in both the linguistic playfulness/delight (*you*) and the wandering/dreaming way of living.

The next movement in God's creation is by means of *differentiation*: "and God separated the light from the darkness. God called the light Day, and the darkness he called Night. And there was evening and there was morning, the first day" (Gen 1:4b–5). Light and darkness, like day and night, are not opposing or antagonistic to each other; darkness is neither

---

15. See Vernon Robbins, *The Invention of Christian Discourse* (Blandford Forum: Deo Publishing, 2009), Vol. 1:179.

16. W. Nicol, *The Semeia in the Fourth Gospel* (NovtSup 32; Leiden: E. J. Brill, 1972), 114.

bad nor evil in relation to light. With the influence of Hellenistic thinking, however, "darkness" in the Gospel of John refers to "the world alienated from God, spiritually ignorant and blind, fallen and sinful, dominated by Satan."[17]

I submit that, in Genesis 1, the Hebraic understanding of "different and yet not opposite" is similar to the "yin-yang" understanding in the classical Chinese worldview.[18] Just as there is a dot of yin (a shadowy or moon-lit spot) in yang (sun-lit spot), so do darkness and night have points of light. We do not know the nature of darkness and night, and they are not the focus of wisdom (at least not conventional wisdom). Yet the biblical text here does not pronounce (or curse) darkness and night as negativity, but rather defines them in terms of distance or separation as a way to respect territory or mark boundaries. A similar dynamic can be seen in the creation of a dome in Genesis 1. The waters above are separated from the waters below, just as the waters under the sky are separated from the dry land (1:6–10); this separation is not based on opposites, but on differentiation and identification. This differentiation also is evident in God's creation of plants yielding seed and fruit trees (1:11–12).

Next is the creation of rhythm and sequence in Genesis 1, as God sets into motion signs, seasons, days, and years (1:14). The dynamic of order is established using differentiation (sun, moon, and stars in 1:16–18) and, on occasion, hierarchical logic (the sun is "the greater light" to rule the day, the moon is "the lesser light" to rule the night; Gen 1:16)—"and God saw that it was good" (Gen 1:18). Even the sea monster, representing the source of chaos, is perceived to be good in the balanced ecology of God's creation.

---

17. Darkness (*skotia*) occurs in John 1:5; 6:17; 8:12; 12:35, 46; 20:1; also see 3:19. Köstenberger, *A Theology of John's Gospel and Letters*, 339. Thus, John's understanding that the darkness has not overcome the light (1:15), though the word "overcome" can be understood less antagonistically as "understood" (NIV), "comprehended" (NASB, NKJV), "extinguished" (NLT), or "mastered" (ISV). Köstenberger is correct in contextualizing John's argument regarding the light and darkness: "For some [of his readers], light was wisdom (or wisdom was even superior to light; cf. Wis 7:26–30). For others, light was given by the Mosaic law (2 Bar 59:2) or Scripture (Ps 19:8; 119:105, 130; Prov 6:23). Still others looked for enlightenment in philosophy, morality, or a simple lifestyle. In this religiously pluralistic context, John proclaims Jesus as the supreme light, who is both eternal and universal and yet personal" (339).

18. See K. K. Yeo, "The 'Yin and Yang' of God (Exod 3:14) and Humanity (Gen 1:27)," *Zeitschrift für Religions-und Geistesgeschichte* 46.4 (1994), 319–332.

Let us revisit the relationship of light and darkness to each other and to the Creator-Light.

A. "Thick darkness" and uncreated Light of God are the dwelling place of God, which does not seem to have the need of differentiation. God dwells in "thick darkness" (*arafel*)—which is His Light (1 Kings 8:12; 2 Chr 6:1; Exo 20:21; Deut 4:11, 5:22; 2 Sam 22:10; Isa 60:2; Ps 18:9; Ps 97:2; Job 38:9). The texts do not assert that God partake of the nature of "thick darkness," but that God has a command of it and can even judge through the thick darkness (Job 22:13).

B. In Genesis 1, God as the super-luminous Light creates light but not darkness. Darkness exists already in the *tohu va-vohu* ("formless void") or ἀόρατος (LXX: *aoratos*, "invisible") of the earth, and darkness covers the face of the abyss (1:2). God's awesome decree echoes over the dark deep, God commands light into being, light obeys and is realized, and God appraises light as good (1:4). But God does not command darkness, although in the presence of light, darkness is now visible (LXX). God does not change the nature of darkness, neither does God command darkness to produce good. Instead, God creates light *out of* darkness, separates light from darkness (1:4), and names darkness "night" (1:5). The separation of light from darkness and the visibility of darkness are *part of the goodness* of creation that God affirms (1:18). It remains a mystery why God does not differentiate things in darkness and why he does not command goodness out of darkness. It is important to note that God *neither names nor sees* darkness as evil. God does not eliminate evil, and this poses a challenge to theodicy regarding God's omnipotence and omnibenevolence.

Both in Genesis and in John, the uncreated Light shines forth God's glory.

II. THE IMAGE AND GOD, ITS SHADOW, AND SPEECH-LIGHT-ACT

Human beings are created to be the "likeness"/ "image" of God-the-Light and the "likeness" of sun-moon-stars-the-light. "Image of God" presupposes the relationship between God and light, specifically God (is) the Light (uncreated). To make the uncreated Light visible, God creates the light, in various forms (sun, moon, stars, etc.). Created light does not produce things; it differentiates them, thus enabling *a context of productivity*, such as that of the waters under the sky (that "bring forth swarms of living creatures" in Gen 1:20) and the earth (that put forth "living creatures of every kind" in Gen 1:24 and vegetation in 1:11).[19] In other words, human beings have a *dual function* in differentiating (as the image of God) and reproducing (as the likeness of sun-moon-stars-light). Light cannot reproduce things; only waters and earth are able to reproduce. But light *rules and enables* waters and earth to produce things from themselves.

Being the enlightened or light-like image of God, Adam and Eve are not created independently, but analogously to their Creator. "Enlightened image" means "shadow" in our contemporary language. We see this in the classical language of Zhuangzi:

> "My shadow is my skin and my wings—
> My aura, my glory, giving me my self.
> Everything in the end interdepends with everything else."[20]

Wu Kuang-min comments that, "'Shadow' is an interesting notion. . . . A man without his shadow is a shadowy existence . . . Why? Because shadow gives a man depth, which makes a man exist, a recognizable existence, perhaps even to himself."[21] A person without a shadow does not live an embodied life; he or she is a ghost. I also find Zhuangzi's understanding of shadow in relation to dream intriguing. He believes that dream is a resource that lures human beings to real life as *wu* ("nothingness") and *you* ("existence") are united;[22] this seems to me similar to the understanding of dreams and visions in the prophetic tradition of the Bible. "In a dream, [is] in a vision of the night" (Job 33:15; Isa 29:7). Dream or vision "is the activity that most powerfully convinces us that we ourselves are

---

19. See Robbins, *The Invention of Christian Discourse*, 135.

20. Wu Kuang-ming, *The Butterfly as Companion: Meditations on the First Three Chapters of the* Chuang Tzu (New York: State University of New York, 1990), 223.

21. Wu, *The Butterfly as Companion*, 223. See Wu's usage of Carl G. Jung's depth psychology to illustrate shadow as that human consciousness hidden in the dark, forgotten corner that we prefer not to see, yet becomes a powerful self once enlightened (brought to consciousness). Zhuangzi, however, speaks of awakening.

22. The most well-known story of Zhuangzi is that of a butterfly dreaming himself. Kuang-ming Wu paraphrases, "Chuang Tzu dreamed of being a butterfly. He suddenly awoke and realized that he was not a butterfly; but then, upon reflection, he was not sure. Was he he who had dreamed of being a butterfly? Or was he a butterfly now dreaming of being he? Thus it was that the butterfly became his companion, in dreaming and in waking, to his life reflections, to his zestful, jestful living." (Wu, *The Butterfly as Companion*, xiii) Butterfly-flutterings in meaning, in irony, in play—in life and death.

part and parcel of the process of interchange among things. That is, we are one among things that mutually change, influence, co-arise, and co-cause one another."[23] Even in God-talk, the concept of shadow is used to denote God's presence. The shadow of God's wings (Ps 17:8; 36:7; 57:1; 63:7; cf. Isa 49:2; 51:16; Lam 4:20; Hos 14:7) is an extension of God's sovereign presence.[24] Moses shall not see the face of God, only God's back (Exo 33:23). Just as God creates light out of darkness for the purpose of differentiation and identification with creation, human beings must have both shadow (darkness) and light in them in order to be authentic.

God's speech-light-act (enlightening) was given to Adam and Eve as a divine gift of naming and seeing. In that regard, they are gifted with the *imitatio Dei* in their speech-light life, i.e., (re)producing goodness in wisdom (light) through their speech-act. In their likeness to the lights of the heavenly bodies (sun, moon, and stars) ruling over the day and the night (Gen 1:18), they are to continue the creative, loving-mercy (*hesed*) of God as tender/manager/steward of the world (*tikkun olam*)—radiating goodness and energizing prosperity in the "dominion" (Gen 1:28) charged to them.

The dominion/ruling/reigning from Genesis 1 is seen later in the biblical texts as re-appropriation of God's wisdom/instruction/law (cf. John 1:17) for the sake of ruling and caring for the created world, especially that of human habitation. Human beings charged with ruling the earth is analogous to the two greater lights in the dome of the sky that "rule over the day and the night" and "separate the light from the darkness" (Gen 1:18). To separate is to use linguistic differentiation, i.e., naming and category. Thus, Adam's naming of animals, of Eve, of Abraham and Joseph, even of God (Exo 3:14), comes close to breaking the second of the 10 commandments—yet the ability to name is a divine gift to the Adamites before the fall.[25]

The naming and enlightening of things, with their intrinsic goodness affirmed, is best exemplified by the rabbi of the Nazareth: "You are the salt of the earth" (Matt 5:13); and "I am the vine, you are the branches" (John 15:5). And the apostle Paul says, "You are the body of Christ"

23. Wu, *The Butterfly as Companion*, 225.

24. Shadow as presence is used in Song 2:3, Isa 30:2 (of Egypt), Acts 5:15 (Peter's shadow). Interesting enough, the "Father of Lights" has no shadow at all (Jam 1:17).

25. For more, see my discussion in *Classical Rhetoric: Greco-Roman Culture and Biblical Hermeneutic* (in Chinese; Hong Kong: Logos and Pneuma, 2002), 117–146.

(1 Cor 12:27). Humans are to be God-like, as in "Be merciful, just as your heavenly Father is merciful" (Luke 6:36). Humans are to be like the sun, moon, and stars, as in "You are the light of the world" (Matt 5:14), as Jesus is the Light of the world (John 1:9, 3:19, 8:12, 9:5, 12:46). Humans are to be like good trees that bear good fruit (Ps 1:3; Matt 6:16–20; Luke 6:43–44). Humans are to be "wise as serpents and innocent as doves" (Matt 10:16).

III. LIGHT AS CREATIVITY AND FRUITFULNESS

Light means creativity/newness, energy/productivity—thus, fruitfulness in various dimensions such as labor, virtue, and meditation. Wisdom (not knowledge, even that of good and evil) itself has long been understood as the tree of life in the garden of Eden (Gen 2:9) and later in the wisdom tradition: "[Wisdom] is a tree of life to those who take hold of her, and happy are all who hold her fast" (Prov 3:18). Thus, the imperative "Be fruitful and multiply" in Genesis 1:28 entails not physical maturity, but the theological-ethical reproduction of goodness so that people as lights of God become "trees of life" to others.

It could be argued that the semantic domain of *martyr* ("witness," "testify")[26] in the Gospel of John is within the realm of light, following the prophetic tradition of the Old Testament with regard to people of God engaging in social justice for the betterment of the world. In John 1:6–9, the author writes:

> [6]There was a man sent from God, whose name was John. [7]He came as a witness (*martyrian*) to testify (*martyrēsēi*) to the light, so that all might believe through him. [8]He himself was not the light, but he came to testify (*martyrēsēi*) to the light. [9]The true light, which enlightens everyone, was coming into the world. (John 1:6–9)

The production of good (fruitfulness) enabled by light (wisdom) is contrasted in later wisdom tradition, not with the production of evil by sin, but contrasted with the multiplication of evil/sin by desire/coveting (*epithymia*). The text of Jacobus/James provides a graphic exegesis. James names God as "Father of Lights" (1:17), who therefore would nei-

---

26. The verb *martyreō* appears 42 times in John (1:7, 8, 15, 32, 34; 2:25; 3:11, 26, 28, 32; 4:39, 44; 5:31, 32, 33, 36, 37, 39; 7:7; 8:13, 14, 18; 10:25; 12:17; 13:21; 15:16, 27; 18:23, 37; 19:35; 21:24), the noun *martyria* appears14 times in John (1:7, 19; 3:11, 32, 33; 5:31, 32, 34, 36; 8:13, 14, 17; 19:35; 21:24).

ther be tempted by evil nor tempt anyone (1:13)—although in principle, God could. And James asserts that "One is tempted by one's own desire" (1:14)—although in theory, one could be tempted by goodness (such as prosperity) as well. That James would pick on the 10th commandment (Exo 20:17; Deut 5:21) is intentional. James speaks of ἐπιθυμία ("desire") as an unending, unsatisfiable quest that *keeps* (present tense) "luring and enticing" (ἐξελκόμενος καὶ δελεαζόμενος) human beings (Jas 1:14).[27] Then James 1:15 graphically uses the concept of birthing to speak of the conception of desire like an embryo/fetus; sin is birthed forth like a child, then the child grown to adulthood gives birth to death. The enthymeme (unstated consensus) of this birthing or reproduction process is in contrast to that of Light (God) producing light (wisdom) producing *imago Dei* (visible Light) producing goodness, producing life, as seen in the Genesis 1 narrative. The state of being that is contrary to the birth of desire in James is given in 1:18: the Father of lights "gave us birth by the word of truth." Thus, human beings are analogous to the "first fruits of his creatures" to whom the earth gave birth enabled by light.

In Hebrew scripture, God's speech-act (enlightening and seeing) in the form of Torah commandments (10 or 613 of them) is revealed to Moses for the purpose of promoting and guiding life into prosperity and fruitfulness. Among many Israelite sages, Solomon collects and writes much proverbial wisdom to guide children and leaders in living productively. John affirms that, "The law indeed was given through Moses; grace and truth came through Jesus Christ" (John 1:17).

The human body, as a microcosm of the cosmic body, contains God's creative wisdom; human beings can and should perceive God's wisdom, meditate on this wisdom of life, and live it in such a way as to produce the goodness that God's wisdom produces. Biblical proverbs exhort people to fear and honor God in order to begin accessing God's wisdom and to employ their bodies—their eyes, ears, hearts, mouths, hands, and feet—to reveal the wisdom of God in the world. In the New Testament, "light," "lamp," and "eyes" are common metaphors used to convey religious and ethical instructions,[28] such as when a family member lights a lamp so that

---

27. Robbins, *The Invention of Christian Discourse*, 158–160.

28. E.g., Luke 11:33–36 (par. 6:22–23), taken from Robbins, *The Invention of Christian Discourse*, 179: [33]No one after lighting a lamp puts it in a cellar, but on the lampstand so that those who enter may see the light. [34]Your eye is the lamp of your body. If your eye is healthy, your whole body is full of light; but if it is not healthy, your body is full of dark-

the household can see the light. God's light is transferred to a person's body, whose eye is then likened to a lamp. Because of God's light/wisdom "enlightening our eyes" (Ps 19:8; "the commandment of the Lord is clear, enlightening the eyes"), a holistic self (health) means one's eye is sound and one's body is full of light. The part of our body that shines out light is the eye.

Light generates life; commandment and teaching produce fruits of goodness. The Book of Proverbs tells us that, "For the commandment is a lamp and the teaching a light, and the reproofs of discipline are the way of life" (6:23). In ethical discourse, people are portrayed as a light that shines brightly: "The light of the righteous shines brightly, but the lamp of the wicked goes out" (Prov 13:9); "But the path of the righteous is like the light of dawn, that shines brighter and brighter until the full day" (Prov 4:18). John constantly speaks of divine friendship that frees Jesus' followers to love one another (John 13:34) and to wash others' feet (John 13).

Prophets are "seers" who guide people in their forth- and fore-telling, so that they may see/understand, repent, and live according to the *ma'at/order*/law of life God has created. Being blind is an infirmity, but neither an evil nor a sin. Jesus heals many blind people,[29] and the famous one is recorded in John 9, which speaks of both physical and spiritual blindness. The worst blindness is a pretense of sight on the part of religious leaders (Matt 25:17; Rom 2:19).

John is very much aware of Isaiah's vision of the coming Messiah as a light to the people: "the people walking in darkness have seen a great light; on those living in the land of deep darkness a light has dawned" (Isa 9:2). Thus, John sees Jesus as the true light of the world (1:12–13, 8:12, 9:5), just as he is the true bread from heaven (John 6:32) and the true vine (15:1). After the sign/miracle of raising Lazarus from death (John 11), Jesus enters Jerusalem for the Passover Festival (John 12:12–15): "The hour has come for the Son of Man to be glorified" (12:20–23). John continues, "You are going to have the light just a little while longer. *Walk* while you have the light, before darkness overtakes you. Those who *walk* in the dark do not know where they are going. Put your trust in the light while you have light, so that you may become *children of light*. . . . I have

---

ness. [35]Therefore consider whether the light in you is not darkness. [36]If then your whole body is full of light, with no part of it in darkness, it will be as full of light as when a lamp gives you light with its rays. (Luke 11:33–36)

29. Matt 9:27–31; 11:5; 12:22; 15:30–31; 20:29–34; 21:14.

come into the world as a light, so that no one who believes in me should stay in darkness" (John 12:35–6).

BIBLICAL PRINCIPLES FOR PROJECT INTERFAITH: IMAG(INATION), FRUITFULNESS, LIFE

The "God as Light" project of this interfaith conference does not prescribe any particular agenda, and I make no attempt in my conclusion to come up with any imperatives. Yet, I believe pretending that different faiths have no assumptions, agendas, or purposes is not helpful to the cause of this Project Interfaith. Thus, I wish to offer a few remarks, suggestive of the ways we may want to move forward in the world of differences, deception, and injustice. I acknowledge the limitations of my scope in this paper in dealing with a selective biblical tradition. It seems to me, though, that rather than living in an inauthentic manner for the sake of "political correctness," I can offer the modest but genuine insight I glean from Genesis and John, and hope that every participant will do likewise from their different texts, cultures, traditions, faiths, etc. Out of my own tradition and examination of Genesis and John, I propose three guiding principles.

1. Method of Imag(ination) (creative dialogue vs. the constraints of a classical paradigm)

    Although my starting point is with the wisdom tradition in the Christian Bible, I do find shared concerns and common insights across space and time. While different faiths may have different contours of understanding and naming of human worth(iness), the meaning of the enlightened/light-like image of God is that which we all can agree on. Without the acknowledgement of God as Light and humans as created light, we would be denying each other our shared worth, making it difficult to engage in dialogue. Creative dialogue is possible, however, if it is based on the acceptance and respect of one another (the whole human race, in fact) as *imago Dei*. Creative dialogue requires that we each know who we are in light of the Creator Light, and be generous enough to bring forth resources from each faith and culture. Without this, dialogues cannot be enlightening or productive. The classical paradigm of interfaith dialogue (inclusivism, exclusivism, pluralism, relativism, and other "isms") may provide some intellectual clarifications. Still, I think a more engaging exchange based on creative imagination of authentic faiths is necessary.

2. Virtue of Goodness (diversity and differentiation/authenticity)

In most interfaith initiatives today, the predominant concern—and the individuals involved—often are those of the Abrahamic faiths (Judaism, Christianity, and Islam). I think this is a short-sightedness that needs vision correction. As I understand "sibling rivalry," it often is more "ugly" and violent than conflicts with individuals outside the family. For this reason, perhaps, the role of intermediary is best served by an arbiter who is not a relative. We need to include in this dialogue Asian faiths (religious, philosophical, ethical, or secular beliefs), indigenous religions, and emerging religions. The goal is neither to provide equal time for each faith to speak, nor to invite equal numbers of participants from each faith tradition. We can ignore artificial measures of equality and, however inequitable it may look on the surface, as conference members, make a commitment based on the virtue of goodness—that is, holding on to the value of diversity and differentiation. Domination, violence, and hatred have no share in the virtue of goodness; diversity does not mean "anything goes." If the glory of God, as narrated in Genesis 1–2, is reflected in the diverse creations of God, goodness refers to the multiplicity of goodness. Multiplicity is not "void and chaos," but a differentiation that will affirm authenticity of different beings and make them interconnect with one another in the great order of life.

3. *Telos* of life-superabundance (realism about challenges faced by humanity and how to overcome destructive powers)

Interfaith dialogue may have a lot of purposes, but I believe one of the primary concerns should be the enhancement of the quality of life. This *telos* of life-superabundance seeks to overcome the common issues threatening the human race today. We do not have the luxury of thinking of disparate, alienated humanities. There is only "one body" of the human race. Wars, poverty, and injustice in one part of the world, one segment of humanity, dehumanize the *whole* human race. To tune out the pain and suffering of people in our own nation and in other countries is to deny the one humanity that is the *imago Dei* in *all* of us. Wisdom literatures (but also, to some extent, prophetic and priestly traditions) often use light and life in that cluster precisely because of the challenges, chaos, and powers of sin, or even evil, that were destroying the life God the Light created. Interfaith conferencing should not begin with the theological question, "Are we worshipping the same God?" The first question should be: "How are we, the light of the world, going to name the darkness and destructive powers in our world today?" Or, "How can we shed light on bringing about life-superabundance through the theological-ethical resources of our faiths?" Religious laws are gifts of God for all children of light to cultivate virtues of goodness, mercy, and justice.

The three dicta of an interfaith project are:

Let there be light.

It is good.

Be fruitful.

K. K. Yeo
Presented at Garrett-Evangelical Theological Seminary
May 1, 2010

PART 2

African and Asian Perspectives

4

'Good Religion' and the Quest for Constructive Inter-religious Dialogue

Larry Murphy

ONE OF THE ANIMATING questions of the "God as Light" conference, that gave rise to this volume, involved the search for a ground upon which adherents to divergent religious traditions might engage in mutually respectful, appreciative dialogue toward some common, constructive ends, as opposed to the all-too-common alternatives of dismissive violence and domination of the "other." There was an implicit assumption recurrent in the conversations of the conference that the source of the hostility lay in the conflicting, incompatible theological tenets of religious systems that encounter one another. I would like to test that assumption and pose, for discussion, an alternative assessment.

My question is whether the creedal/theological/philosophical formulations of the world's religions are the source of the conflicts and attendant acts of violence and domination amongst peoples or, rather, are the after-the-fact constructions of rationales and justifications for doing what people are wont to do, regardless. Is there in the make-up, the nature, of the human being or the human enterprise that conduces or constrains persons to acts of aggression or, alternatively, to acts of care and mutuality? Both seem equally compelling and pervasive. Could these two vectors of human behavior be rooted in fundamental survival and security instincts, paired with what neuroscientists tell us is our human "hard-wiring" for association in supportive human community? Thus, is either of these behaviors *dependent* on the teachings of faith traditions? Or may they, perhaps, significantly inform the ideational/theological formulations of faith traditions? Comments from various persons in one of the conference sessions described fundamental theological tenets and canonical texts among the various religious traditions which, in effect, sacralized what peoples had already done, or were presently engaged in doing, whether from survival concerns, or pursuing an aspiration, or satisfying a compulsion or a "consuming passion." This is not to suggest that theologies are simply or solely arbitrary, justifying covers for human willfulness. Rather, it is an effort to probe the relationship between genuine theological discernment, the perspectival particularity of the articulation of that which is apprehended, and the givens of our human propensities to act.

Over recent decades, some students of African-American religious history have written that enslaved Africans in the U.S. embraced Christianity because it provided transcendent existential affirmation, asserted God's concern for justice, and thereby validated liberative action. Black Theology, as developed over the years and formalized by latter-day theological scholars, is said to be the coalescence of this line of thought, generating prophetic societal critique and civil rights protest. But is not the will to freedom from arbitrary, oppressive constraint a natural endowment, i.e., *Sui generis*? Do not the oppressed seek liberation apart from/regardless of religion's claims, the latter providing the hermeneutical articulation of primal inclinations, grounding them, *ex post facto*, in transcendent authority? Likewise, was the subjugation of the African, of the Native American, or other historically colonized groups merely to be seen as fulfillment of biblical mandates or obedient implementation of creedal directives?

If one is genuinely a person of religious faith, hermeneutical constructions that fund such actions could well be integrous discernments of the divine will, while yet leaving open the theo-anthropological issue of the relationship of the divine will to primal human inclinations—positive and negative (e.g., divine will as the source, through Creation, or not). If there is any merit in the line of inquiry I am raising, then would not the way forward to constructive inter-religious dialogue have to begin by discernment of the forces that motivate us, that give us shared interests and those that also put us in contested spaces, then explore how our religious constructions frame these? In so doing, could we not trace back through these constructions to those core issues around which we could have dialogue *that matters*, around the things that are *really* at stake, toward which our religious mythoi and doctrinal formulations are but signposts?

To be sure, the claim to transcendent truth asserted by religious systems, especially those that assert the universality and exclusivity of their truth, poses a challenge to any meaningful, fruitful *dialogue*. Perhaps the necessary first step, the *sine qua non* of dialogue, per se, is the willingness to entertain the notion—if only for discussion—that adherents to other modes of belief and devotion may, nonetheless, be adherents to what, if not complete and fully adequate by one's standards, is at least "good religion."

In an article entitled "Good Religion, Spirituality, and African Americans," New York Theological Seminary professor Dr. Harold Dean Trulear discerns in the lyrics of the Negro Spiritual "Have You Got Good Religion?" some norms for answering the song's titular query, norms "by which religious faith and its expressions may be judged, evaluated, and critiqued—perhaps even rejected."[1]

Trulear suggests that "good religion" involves "thinking that enables one to revisualize life under the auspices, care, and, even, superintendency of God"—however one's God is named or conceived. Secondly, "'good religion' is interpersonal . . . it can be discerned in the treatment human beings give one another." It is rooted in an inclusive love of humankind that is not boundaried by group identity nor "social convention." Undergirding both these norms," says Trulear, is the element of "transcendence . . . the capacity to imagine beyond the self and its own desires and interests," beyond the contingencies of human predicament and one's given social reality.

Could not "good religion," as it points to the transcendence that seems to be common in religious experience, be that which effectively illumines our nature and the relationship of God to that nature, in ways that enable us to situate all persons, indeed all of Creation, in a structure of shared meaning, in which *dialogue* is not only the only reasonable option but the one we desire and embrace?

Larry Murphy
May 12, 2010

---

1. Harold Dean Trulear, "Good Religion, Spirituality, and African Americans," in *Cross Currents*, 46:4 (Winter 1996–97), http://www.crosscurrents.org/Trulear.html.

5

Violence and Obscurity

Religious Cosmology of Seeing and Hearing in the West African Rainforest

William Murphy

The man who laughs has simply not yet heard the terrible news.
—Bertolt Brecht

INTRODUCTION

INVOKING BERTOLT BRECHT'S POEM about another particularly dark time of violent politics is a rather melancholy beginning for a paper given at a conference on the spiritual radiance of light in interfaith dialogue. The first line of the poem called "To Those Born Later" reads: "Truly, I live in dark times!" In this poem Brecht confronts the "dark times" of his own historical moment of the 1930s, especially the threat of Nazism in Europe. The poem captures a somber mood of the times by drawing attention to this terrible news. Today we confront our own terrible news —whether the news is coming from the wars in Iraq, Afghanistan, the eastern Congo, or whether the news is about violence—both physical and structural—against those defined as outcasts in our own society.

This melancholy note evokes an appropriate beginning for an argument that conceptualizes light in its dialectical relationship with darkness, and pose questions about the political use of this dialectic to create social exclusions based on differentiating those in the light from those in the dark—i.e., those who claim to know religious truth and those who are treated as ignorant of this truth.

This dialectical approach is also congruent with the ethnographic fact that the cultural symbol of light in most religious cosmologies documented by anthropologists is largely structured by opposition with the category of "darkness." As we know from the structuralist analysis of cultural categories used in the narratives, poetry, and rituals of every society, particular dichotomies and antitheses, like light and darkness, provide cultural building blocks for organizing cultural meaning and religious symbolism. In addition, the organizing principle is expanded by various mediations and transformations of initial oppositions, building a richness and complexity of meaning in cultural texts (such as building triadic structures of binary categories mediated by third categories).

To give an example: the opposition of light and darkness may be mediated by the category that is "in between," such as the category of "shadow." Or, to use another obvious instance, the opposition of "male" and "female" in a cultural narrative may be mediated by an "in between" category, such as "androgeny."[1] In addition, variants in cultural narratives are often structured by transformations of invariant dualisms. For example, if "a woman kills her son in one variant, the theme might be inverted so that the son kills his mother in another."[2]

These parallel structures are fundamental formal devices for building the flow of meaning in poetry and narratives, whether in sacred texts or folklore. The texture of ancient Hebrew poetry in the bible, for example, is characteristically shaped by this parallelism, a point emphasized in the foundational inquiry on this poetic form by Robert Lowth in the 18th century. Lowth recognized a kind of grammar to biblical poetry that was based on different sorts of parallel structures, including structures built by antithetical lines of opposed terms.[3]

The contemporary biblical scholar, Robert Alter, has expanded our understanding of the pervasiveness of "semantic parallelism" in narrative and poetic structures of biblical texts. Besides the biblical parallelism built on linked synonymous ideas and images, there is the other important form built on the principle of contrast or opposition, a kind of

---

1. Wendy Doniger, *Myth and Meaning: Cracking the Code of Culture. Claude Levi-Strauss* (New York: Schocken Books, 1995), viii.

2. Ibid., xiv.

3. Roman Jakobson, "Grammatical Parallelism and Its Russian Facet," in *Language in Literature*, Krystyna Pormorska and Stephen Rudy, eds. (Cambridge: Harvard University Press, 1987), 146.

"antithetical symmetry" of the type embodied in the phraseology, "man proposes, God disposes."[4] The imagery of light and darkness is constructed in biblical texts through this antithetical parallelism of oppositions, including homologous pairs of oppositions, e.g., day vs. night or morning vs. evening.

The first psalm is one of the many examples Alter[5] uses to illustrate the tight logical structure of antithetical parallelism:

> For the Lord embraces the way of the righteous
> And the way of the wicked is lost.

The content of this parallelism could be diagrammed by listing the oppositions which are the building blocks of meaning in this poetic expression:

- Righteous/wicked
- Embraced/lost

Alter also analyzes the Book of Proverbs as an especially rich text, which builds meaning through recurrent images divided into "antithetical clusters," such as the key image of a path or way as "smooth or straight."[6] "Other frequent figurative antitheses are riches and jewels against poverty; life and healing over against death and sickness; sweetness and honey . . . over against bitterness and wormwood; light against darkness."[7] The important analytical point here is that the "flow of meaning" in biblical texts "is channeled in the system of poetic parallelism," including antithetical meanings.[8] The importance of semantic parallelism helps us recognize that the meaning of the religious symbol of light is largely built through poetic, parallel structures of opposition with darkness.

Besides biblical scholarship, the structuralist emphasis on cultural oppositions and their mediations and transformations in structures of meaning-making in a community became a theoretical emphasis in social and cultural theory developed and made most famous by the an-

---

4. Robert Alter, *Genesis: Translation and Commentary* (New York: W.W. Norton, 1996), 47.
5. Robert Alter, *The Art of Biblical Poetry* (New York: Basic Books, 1985), 115.
6. Ibid., 170–71.
7. Ibid., 171.
8. Ibid., 18.

thropologist, Claude Levi-Strauss.⁹ But the key methodological challenge in anthropological study is to move beyond structural assumptions by asking questions about how particular oppositions and their mediations function in people's everyday lives—especially, how the opposition which differentiates something in nature—e.g., light and darkness—is used in the language of social life to differentiate people, i.e., those in the light and those in the dark. The further question is how natural oppositions representing social differentiations are used as a method of social exclusion and domination in the political life of a society —and even used as ideological means for justifying violence against those in the "dark."

The cross-cultural case of using natural oppositions, especially involving seeing and hearing, to build a religious cosmology of social differentiations in societies of the West African rainforest will be included in this essay as further evidence of this fundamental grammar of religious poetics and its implications for the politics of social differentiation in a community. The dialectical question of light and darkness will be pursued by considering related cultural homologies, especially knowledge/ignorance—but also other homologies, such as white/black in colonialist discourse in Africa or male/female in religious gender hierarchies (i.e., men are pure vs. women are impure, or men have reason vs. women have emotions). The concept of homology here is meant to capture the idea that these different cultural oppositions share a similarity because they serve the same ideological function of defining the social separation of those illuminated with true knowledge and those living in the darkness of ignorance. Consider first the biblical homology of light and darkness as representing knowledge and ignorance.

LIGHT AND DARKNESS, KNOWLEDGE, AND IGNORANCE

This opposition of light and darkness is explicit and pervasive organizing principle in Judaeo-Christian biblical passages. We could cite numerous examples, but briefly consider three. The beginning of the bible, in the book of Genesis, begins with this opposition:

> And God said, Let there be light: and there was light.
> And God saw the light, that it was good: and God divided the light from the darkness.

---

9. Claude Levi-Strauss, *The Raw and the Cooked* (Chicago: University of Chicago, 1983).

This dialectic is repeated throughout the bible, in St. Paul, for example, in 2 Corinthian 4:6, in which Jesus Christ becomes the fulfillment of bringing "light" in the world: "For God, who commanded the light to shine out of darkness, hath shined in our hearts, give light of the knowledge of the glory of God in the face of Jesus Christ." In other words, when God created the heaven and earth he brought "light."

In John we get the dialectical motif again, when Jesus spoke to the people and said, "I am the light of the world. Whoever follows me will never walk in darkness, but will have the light of life" (John 8:12). The opposition is clear: if you have "light" you will not "walk in darkness." Light is a metaphor for the illumination that divine knowledge brings to the world. The homology links "light" and "darkness" to the opposition of "knowledge" vs. "ignorance.

Such biblical texts—and many others—provide a foundation for a theology of light, namely, light as symbolizing the illumination of knowledge, and, in this theological context, the knowledge comes as a gift from God. This theological principle, for example, is found in Thomas Aquinas's *Summa Theologiae*: the light of intelligence that our intellects achieve is a created participation in the eternal and uncreated light of God.[10]

The phenomenological grounding of the symbol of light in this theological framework—or any religious cosmological code—is built on the biological and physical facts of the experience of the human sensory, perceptual apparatus of seeing. We all have experienced going into a dark room and realizing that we cannot distinguish anything, we can't see where the chair, or where the table is. And on the table we can't see the "green" apple and distinguish it from the "red" apple. But once the light is turned on, we can make all these relevant distinctions that are important for our life, and even our survival.

Light is thus a natural symbol for being able to discern, distinguish, and thus to see the differences between things. And it provides religious cosmologies with a powerful symbol of knowledge—for the illumination of understanding as a spiritual gift. Divination practices in Africa, for example, build on this cosmology of knowing a "forest of symbols" as a

---

10. Bernard Lonergan. *Understanding and Being* (Collected Works of Bernard Lonergan, Vol. 5), Elizabeth A. Morelli and Mark D. Morelli, eds. (Toronto: University of Toronto, 1990), 390.

source of insight and illumination.[11] But as used in the social life of communities, illumination is also a powerful symbol for differentiating those who lack this special knowledge.

It is important to note that this cultural logic of knowledge and ignorance represented by the opposition of light and darkness has also divided the Abrahamic family of religions, especially through the homology of "spirit" and "flesh." In one common textual form of this opposition, for example, Islam develops as a religious heritage from Ishmael, one of Abraham's sons, who is associated with the ignorance of the "flesh," while the other son, Isaac, is associated with the correct knowledge of the spirit transmitted to the true religion of Christianity. In St. Paul's epistles, the contrast of spirit and flesh is a key motif, providing a binary opposition for separating Christians from Jews. Jews, in the cultural logic, have not yet transcended the flesh, but still lack the true spirit of God and the Holy Spirit of Christianity. Conversion, for St. Paul, replaces the ignorance of the flesh with the light of the spirit of God. (The paragraph above is based on Professor Souleymane Bachir Diagne's comment after my workshop presentation in which he drew attention to the related logic and politics of the opposition of "spirit" and "flesh" in Abrahamic religious debates and divisions. His comment added a necessary historical reality and rhetorical complexity to interfaith dialogue.)

SEEING AND HEARING IN BIBLICAL NARRATIVE

Two additional, key oppositions in biblical narratives provide further homologies of the differentiation of those who know from those who do not know. One opposition is the distinction between those who see but do not perceive; the second is those who hear but do not understand. In both cases, these oppositions are homologous with the distinction of those in the light and those in the dark.

These two oppositions are often used together in biblical texts to express the parallelism of an antithesis between those who know and those who do not know. Consider briefly three representative passages. In Ezekiel 12:2, we learn of those rebellious people who "have eyes to see, but see not, who have ears to hear, but hear not." Similarly in Mark 4:12, see-

---

11. Victor Turner, *The Forest of Symbols: Aspects of Ndembu Ritual* (Ithaca: Cornell University, 1967); cf. René Devisch, *Weaving the Threads of Life: The Khita Gyn-Eco-Logical Healing Cult Among the Yaka* (Chicago: University of Chicago, 1993).

ing and hearing are homologous pairs for representing ignorance: "while seeing, they may see and not perceive, and while hearing, they may hear but not understand." Finally, in Matthew 13:14, we learn that as much as they try the hard-headed will not understand, as Isaiah had prophesized: "you will keep on hearing, but will not understand; you will keep on seeing, but will not perceive." This homology of knowledge and ignorance related to seeing and hearing is found many other biblical passages.

The dialectic of light and darkness, as differentiating those who know from those who do not know, becomes reinforced in biblical texts by the homologies of seeing but not perceiving and hearing but not understanding. In this oppositional logic, there are also those who see and perceive properly, and those who hear and understand. They are the people who understand the truth, who have the illumination of true knowledge as a spiritual gift.

TRANSFORMATION: LIGHT IS GOOD/LIGHT IS EVIL

God in Genesis saw that "light" was good, with the implication that darkness—and ignorance—is bad. But could light be bad and darkness good in some cultural logics? The empirical challenge, of course, is finding the expression and realization of such transformations in the narratives and cultural symbolism of a particular society.

But one further logical transformation—namely, the opposition in which light as good is contrasted with light as evil—can be found can be found in various cultural codes of different societies. Two examples from Western art can exemplify this transformation. Both examples concern the symbol of light as related to war and violence: Goya's "3rd May, 1808" and Picasso's "Guernica."

Goya's painting depicts the execution in Madrid of rebels who had arisen against Napoleon's invasion of Spain. The execution takes place at night, producing a painting of a scene "in which the dirty business is being done" by the light of a lantern, which enables the evil deed.[12] "Goya's terrible fancy" in this depiction reminds us that 'modern light might also be malign—the enabler of torture and murder.'"[13]

Another scene of violence from a different period of war in the same country is depicted in Picasso's "Guernica." In this instance, the violence

12. Simon Schama, *The Power of Art* (London: BBC Books, 2006), 383.
13. Ibid., 383.

is the bombing, on April 26, 1937, of the defenseless Basque town of Guernica. The bombing was carried out by the German allies of Franco's army in the Spanish civil war. In this painting, Picasso "stands the conventions of art themselves on their head" by transforming the symbol of light as a source of goodness and beauty—i.e., a long Western painting tradition of light as spiritual radiance, and paintings, such as those by Caravaggio or Rembrandt, as "emitting light." Now the light in the painting—a light bulb at the center of Guernica is an "implacable incandescence beneath which the horse writhes in its death throes and shrieking mayhem proceeds," another representation of "brightly illuminated modern miseries."[14] Right next to the evil-eyed light bulb is a "candle-light, held out by a classically beautiful arm," producing at the center of the painting "a tournament of light . . . good and wicked."[15] The bright light bulb of the torturer's cell or the searchlight of the bomber contrasts, in the symbolism of modern war and violence, with the luminous light emitting beauty and goodness.

The variety of potential meanings in any set of contrasting symbols, such as light and darkness, generate logical transformations shaping the narratives, poetry, art, and rituals of a community. The core structuralist issue for the analysis of any cultural symbolism is how the process of meaning-making in such texts operates through a poetics of oppositions and their transformation. But the further question is how those meanings are used in specific contexts to inform the daily lives people lead, especially how the meanings structure the politics of social exclusions and subordinations in a community. The poetics of oppositions in religious texts are often transformed into the politics of social oppositions in a community—a theoretical theme addressed in the next section.

POETICS OF CULTURAL OPPOSITIONS AS POLITICS OF SOCIAL EXCLUSION

The key anthropological question about any set of oppositions, homologies, and transformations in the symbolic and narrative universe of a religion is how these symbolic elements are used in social and political life to create meanings and justifications for differentiating people in society, and even justifying the social subordination of the people differentiated.

---

14. Ibid., 383.
15. Ibid., 387.

As we have learned from Durkheim's[16] sociology of religion, with its paradigmatic opposition of the "sacred" and the "profane"—and later through analytical refinements in Levi-Strauss (and many other anthropologists, such as Mary Douglas[17]—the natural symbols of a religion function to differentiate social categories and social relations in a community.

The sensory world provides human beings with the concrete elements for constructing a cultural and religious universe of meanings, as well as a set of social meanings.

But the further lesson—and one that Foucault[18] emphasized in his approach to cultural categories—is that the oppositions in any cultural system—e.g., purity vs. impurity—provide a technique of power as well as a political language for excluding and subordinating some people in the society, e.g., separating those categorized as "mad" vs. sane, or "sinners" vs. the righteous. Power is related to knowledge in this social logic because those with authoritative claims to expert knowledge use that knowledge to legitimate the use of categories to socially separate and exclude—as well as control and discipline. Society, in this analytical approach, is conceptualized as various discursive regimes composed of authoritative forms of language and categories used to exclude and dominate. For the argument here, the opposition of light and darkness and its various homologies provide a cultural resource for a discursive regime of authoritative social separation, exclusion, and subordination.

This analytical principle can be illustrated by the case of the use of light and darkness as an important ideological motif justifying the colonial project in Africa. Colonial officers as well as missionaries were confident in their mission of bringing the light of civilization and Christianity to the black peoples of a continent characterized by ignorance. This confidence and the stereotypes of the opposition of the West and Africa was supported by an ideology constructed from biblical motifs and the homologous oppositions generated from those motifs.

---

16. Emile Durkheim, *The Elementary Forms of the Religious Life*, Karen E. Fields, trans. (New York: Free Press, 1994 [1912]).

17. Mary Douglas, *Purity and Danger: An Analysis of Concepts of Pollution and Taboo* (London: Routledge and K. Paul, 1966).

18. Michel Foucault, *Madness and Civilization: a History of Insanity in the Age of Reason* (New York: Pantheon, 1965); *The History of Sexuality: An Introduction* (Vol. 1) (New York: Vintage, 1990); *Discipline and Punish: the Birth of the Prison* (New York: Vintage, 1995).

The homologous oppositions derived from biblical poetics became part of the language and discourse legitimating colonialism. The core theme was bringing "light to the dark continent," but this opposition of light and darkness took on many transformations in the ideological constructions of colonialism in Africa. One key transformation was white/black: the civilized white man was going to bring light to the uncivilized black. Gender became another homologous opposition, especially with connotations of sexuality: colonialist ideology "reduced Africa to the body of a black female yielding herself to white male discovery."[19] The darkness of the dark continent was thus constructed with provocative imagery of sexuality and emotional excess. Missionary accounts of the civilizing mission of colonialism are filled with theme of the white man's gaze on the "dark heathenism" of Africa—a gaze that records many forms of darkness, such as uncontrolled sexuality, that must be confronted and reformed with the light of Christianity, with all its symbolism of looking and transparency.[20]

The motif of Western man bringing light to the Dark Continent became ideologically mapped out in a political discourse of homologous oppositions, involving race, gender, knowledge, sexuality, emotions, etc. And some of the best evidence of the light/darkness motif is the accounts of missionaries as they proudly portray their role of bringing light of Christianity to the "dark continent"—a "dark continent" needing the light of Christianity.[21]

Consider some key oppositions in this colonial ideological code:

- Light/darkness
- White/black
- Knowledge/ignorance
- Truth/error
- Spirit/flesh
- Male/female
- Reason/emotions

19. Jean Comaroff and John Comaroff, *Of Revelation and Revolution: Christianity, Colonialism and Consciousness in South Africa* (Vol. 1) (Chicago: University of Chicago, 1991), 104.
20. Ibid., 174.
21. Ibid., Chapter 5.

- Civilized/savage
- Tame/wild
- Moral/immoral
- Superior/inferior

It is clarifying to add another homologous opposition that draws its poetic effect from the sounds of the French language—namely, the contrast of *penser* and *danser*—which is often used to differentiate Western and African epistemologies. In this cultural logic, the white man approaches the world by "thinking" (*penser*) and the black African understands the world by "dancing" (*danser*). The opposition of "thinking" and "dancing" provides a homologous refashioning of the opposition of reason and emotions.[22]

Thinking and dancing for the colonial imagination was homologous with the paradigmatic contrast of light/darkness of biblical cosmology as well as related oppositions, all of which provided the ideological foundation of colonialism in Africa.

CASE STUDY: RELIGIOUS COSMOLOGY OF SEEING AND HEARING IN THE WEST AFRICAN RAINFOREST

Methodologically, it is important to document accurately for each culture and community how the language of oppositions like light and darkness are invoked in the daily lives of people to regulate the social differentiations and relations. This general methodological principle was important in the later work of Wittgenstein on the use of language and cultural concepts in everyday situations. In this methodological orientation, Wittgenstein liked to compare himself to anthropologists studying different cultures and foreign communities. Anthropology, in this guise, could be used as a philosophical technique of imagining societies and cultures different from your own in order to clarify what is easily overlooked because too easily taken for granted in your own society and cultural practices. "Imagine," Wittgenstein[23] asked in one of his many thought experiments

---

22. For Senghor's use of *danser* and *penser* in his philosophy and African aesthetics, see Souleymane Bachir Diagne, *Léopard Sédar Senghor: l'art africain comme philosophe* (Paris: Riveneuve, 2007).

23. Ludwig Wittgenstein, *Remarks on Colour*, G.E.M. Anscombe, ed. (Berkeley: University of California, 1977), 4e.

about other cultures, "a tribe of color-blind people . . . it would be difficult for us to translate their color words into ours." The larger question for Wittgenstein is to imagine how the people of this "tribe" carried out their lives without a sense of color or the use of "color words," and how they would talk about and categorize a world in which you could not distinguish between a green apple from a red apple.[24]

This Wittgenstein example of imagining another culture and society provides a useful introduction to a concrete anthropological case in which the sensory world of the rainforest shapes the experience of seeing and hearing as building blocks for a religious cosmology of natural oppositions and social differentiations. The case concerns communities living in the rainforest of Liberia, West Africa, where I have done my anthropological fieldwork. Communities live in carved out clearings of villages in the rainforest, which is interpreted as "an icon of what can be heard but not seen, what can be sensed but not fully understood, and what is felt as present but hidden"[25]—and in general see the rainforest as the locus of spiritual forces in the world. The following example and brief commentary is taken from an article on the rainforest as a source of mystery and secret religious rituals.[26] One day a secret association announced throughout the village that in the evening they would perform a ritual of cleansing the town of witches. The announcement was also a warning that all the women and uninitiated males had to stay inside their houses while this ritual was performed. So like the other non-members I went into the house where I was staying and closed the shutters in my room and waited. You could hear sounds but not see what was going on. The evening was filled with many sounds, especially beautiful were the initial sounds of a beautiful, high-pitched voice calling out from a distance towards a hill next to the village. The first call was faraway, then a later, closer call sounded, and then a third call closer still, as if this singer—or source of the sound—and the group accompanying the sound were proceeding to the village. One meaning of the sound for everyone was the sense that this ritual group was slowly proceeding towards the village. Finally, there was a call right outside the village, followed by the loud noises of what sounded like people rushing into and around the village, stomping the

24. Ibid., 40e.
25. William P. Murphy, "Geometry and Grammar of Mystery: Ancient Mystery Religions and West African Secret Societies" in *Electronic Antiquity* 12:1 (2008), 176.
26. Ibid., 177.

ground and shouting with agitation. These noises, I was told later, represented the men of this secret association fighting with and driving out the witches from the village.

This scene of secret ritual activity raises important questions about the relationship between the visual and auditory in religious practices—namely, what cannot be seen can be heard, and what is heard is intended to communicate the presence of religious activity and mysterious, spiritual forces. There is a special aura of wonder, awe, and fear—a kind of religious sublime—evoked by hearing but not seeing a ritual. And those controlling the ritual have an interest in communicating the message that they are trafficking with extraordinary, spiritual forces. The dialectic of hearing but not seeing indexes the mysterious presence of spiritual forces, and represents a religious performativity of power and authority, as well as knowledge. In other words, the ritual aesthetics of obscurity associated with the rainforest provided the cultural means for creating a religious cosmology of the sublime,[27] as well as a politics of controlling knowledge of the sublime.[28]

This politics is built on the religious cosmological opposition of hearing and not seeing as an ideological resource for building social hierarchies within the community by separating the elders who "know" from the youth in the "dark," as well as separating men from women, or members of high-ranking kinship groups (i.e., those who control ritual practice) from low-ranking kinship groups.[29] These exclusions also play out in the modern context in which the local broker who knows how to mediate with the distant, and often mysterious, doings of the national government is culturally constructed in the homologous image of the religious broker with the mysterious forces of the rainforest.[30] In the context of the civil war in Liberia and Sierra Leone, the religious broker with the rainforest provided spiritual resources of protection and power to the

---

27. William P. Murphy, "Review of *Secrecy: African Art that Conceals and Reveals*" in *African Arts* 27 (1994), 74–76.

28. William P. Murphy, "The Sublime Dance of Mende Politics: An African Aesthetic of Charismatic Power" in *American Anthropologist* 25:4 (1997), 563–582.

29. William P. Murphy, "Secret Knowledge as Property and Power in Kpelle Society: Elders Versus Youth" in *Africa* 50 (1980), 193–207.

30. William P. Murphy, "The Rhetorical Management of Dangerous Knowledge in Kpelle Brokerage" in *American Anthropologist* 8 (1981), 667–685.

combatants in the rebel groups.[31] Religious leaders are "those who know" how to access the spiritual forces of the rainforest, and this knowledge in the context of civil war provide motivation, confidence, and justification for the violence.

In summary, the rainforest sensory world of seeing and hearing provides a religious cosmology with the ideological potential for creating hierarchy and legitimacy based on claims to knowledge with a patriarchical and gerontocratic system. One might add that in contemporary international politics the dialectic of light and darkness is a significant discursive régimes for justifying national and religious exceptionalism, as well as recruiting youth into projects of violence against those in the dark.

CONCLUSION

I will end the essay on a less melancholy note, by invoking some other lines from another Brecht poem, about the human hope and responsibility of speaking and writing—and "singing"—in order to illuminate the violence and injustices in our era.

> In the dark times
> Will there also be singing?
> Yes, there will also be singing
> About the dark times.

The writing about dark times in this essay drew attention to the potential (and actual) use of the religious symbol of "light" to culturally construct social exclusion and subordination by categorizing some people as in the "dark"—and to legitimate violence against the intransigence and evil of those in the "dark" because they fail to see the light (of our religion, our culture, our civilization, etc.). Orchestrators and entrepreneurs of violence often use such antithetic categorizations to strategically substi-

---

31. Stephen Ellis, The Mask of Anarchy: *The Destruction of Liberia and the Religious Dimension of an African Civil War* (New York: New York University Press, 1999); Paul Richards, *Fighting for the Rain Forest: War, Youth and Resources in Sierra Leone* (London: James Currey, 1996); William P. Murphy, "Military Patrimonialism and Child Soldier Clientalism in the Liberian and Sierra Leonean Civil Wars" in *African Studies Review* 46 (2003), 61–87.

tute opposed, singular religious identities in place of a shared, common humanity.[32]

A focus on the poetics of the dialectic of light and darkness reveals the paradox and ambivalence of the symbol of light: the symbol bestows clarity and certainty on the justification of violence against those in the dark. But the "singing" in dark times—whether expressed in the form of painting, poetry, theology, and anthropology, etc.—can illuminate this inherent paradoxical potential of turning the religious poetics of light into a politics of darkness

ACKNOWLEDGEMENTS

I want to thank Ken Vaux for inviting me to participate in the dialogue of this workshop on the religious symbol of light, and to both Ken and Sara Vaux for providing a commune of stimulating conversations on all things human under the sun. I am also grateful to Jean Comaroff's bibliographical suggestions related to Christianity and African colonialism, and to Soulemayne Bachir Diagne for his characteristic clarity and insights on these logical issues of religious meaning.

William Murphy
Presented at Garrett-Evangelical Theological Seminary
May 1, 2010

---

32. Amartya Sen, *Identity and Violence: the Illusion of Destiny* (New York: W. W. Norton, 2006).

6

Light and Sight in the Hindu Tradition and the Faiths of India

Wendy Doniger

THIS ARTICLE WILL COMPARE two rather contradictory attitudes to light and sight in two different parts of Hinduism. One part, the philosophical part, stretching back to the Upanishads, took vision as the primary metaphor for intellectual error: you could not trust any of your senses, but most of all you could not trust your eyes. The other part, the Hinduism of temple worship and sacrifice, of myth and ritual, the dominant form of Hinduism, privileged sight and seeing as the most powerful instrument a human being could have in reaching god. It's most likely that the philosophical tradition came first, the temple worship later, and I will consider them in that order. But in fact, after the first few centuries, they grew up side by side and continued to spur one another on.

VEDANTA PHILOSOPHY OF LIGHT

Indian philosophy made the image of *false* seeing—of mistaking a rope for a snake, or a piece of shell for a piece of silver—an enduring trope for the larger mistake of taking the visual world to be the real world.[1] The philosophy in question here was Vedanta, the philosophical school that reads the Upanishads through the lens of the unity of the Self (*atman*) and the cosmic principle (*brahman*). Often expressing their ideas in the form of commentaries on the Upanishads, on the *Gita*, and on

---

1. Wendy Doniger O'Flaherty, *Dreams, Illusion, and Other Realities* (Chicago: University of Chicago Press, 1984).

Badarayana's *Vedanta Sutras* (c. 400 b.c.e.), different branches of Vedanta tend to relegate the phenomenal world to the status of an epistemological error (*avidya*), a psychological imposition (*adhyaya*), or a metaphysical illusion (*maya*). Evil, too, that the myths struggle to deal with, and, especially, death, turn out to be nothing but an illusion.

Unlike other topics that only erudite Indian philosophers wrestled with, illusion got into the very fabric of Hindu culture, so that just about everyone in the tradition knows about *maya* and the difficulty of telling a snake from a rope. *Maya* is what is made, artificial, constructed, something that seems to be there but has no substance; it is the path of rebirth, in contrast with the path of freedom from rebirth. It is magic, cosmic sleight of hand. The god Indra (the Indian counterpart of Zeus, Jupiter, Odin, Wotan) is the first great magician: magic is called "Indra's Net" (*indra-jala*). At a moment when he is losing a fight, Indra magically turns himself into the hair of one of his horses' tails. Magic illusions of various sorts play a crucial role in the great Sanskrit epics.

The belief that vision was in some way tainted was supported by the mythology in which demons, in particular, were visually unreliable, shape-shifters. It was believed that demons had the ability to project false images, illusions; but the magic project worked only as long as the demon concentrated on making it work. If the person casting the illusion was overcome by lust, or fell asleep, or, above all, when he died, he would no longer be able to go on projecting the false picture show, and would unconsciously assume his true form

The *Kamasutra* (5.6: 24–25)[2] assumes a theory of vision as projection from the eyes when it tells you how to make yourself invisible: put the ointment on your own eyes:

He makes his shadow and his body disappear by means of the magic trick using this technique: He cooks the heart of a mongoose, the fruits of a fenugreek plant and a long gourd, and snake eyes, over a fire that does not smoke. Then he rubs into this the same measure of the collyrium used as eye makeup. When he has smeared his eyes with this, he can move about without a shadow or a body.

Nilakantha's 17th century commentary on the Sanskrit epic, the *Mahabharata*, says that eyeglasses are distorting. The idea is that if you

---

2. *The Kamasutra of Vatsyayana*, trans. Wendy Doniger and Sudhir Kakar (London and New York: Oxford World Classics, 2002).

have bad eyesight, the blurry way you see the world is what is real for you; the lenses distort your vision by making it sharp.

DARSHAN AND LIGHT

Against this deeply ingrained Indian cultural habit of mistrusting your eyes, another branch of Hinduism developed a diametrically opposite view, in which vision was the key to true understanding. This form of Hinduism seemed to assume that god came in at the eye, like love in William Butler Yeats' poem, "A Drinking Song":

> Wine comes in at the mouth
> And love comes in at the eye;
> That's all we shall know for truth
> Before we grow old and die.
> I lift the glass to my mouth,
> I look at you, and sigh.

This aspect of Hinduism paid great attention to sight and seeing, which they called *darshan*.[3] *Darshan*, "seeing," was known throughout North and South India, from the time of the great South Indian saints, Alvars and Nayanmars, in about the 6th century c.e. *Darshan* was the means by which favor passed from one to the other of each of the parties linked by the gaze. One takes *darshan* of a king or a god, up close and personal. *Darshan* is a concept that comes to the world of the temple from the world of the royal court. A feudal king, subject to a superior ruler, had to appear in person in the court of his overlord, publicly affirming his obedient service through a public demonstration of submission, so that he could see and be seen. So, too, the temple was both the god's private dwelling and a palace, a public site where people could not only offer worship but look at the deity and be looked at by him. Many temples have annual processions in which the central image of the god is taken out and carried around the town in a wooden chariot (*rath*), in clear imitation of a royal procession.

To see the deity, therefore, and to have him (or her) see you, was to make possible a transfer of power. And this was the intimate transference that South Indian *bhakti* (passionate devotion) imagined for the god and the worshipper. *Darshan* may also have been inspired, in part,

---

3. Diana L. Eck, *Darsan: Seeing the Divine Image in India* (New York: Columbia University Press, 1996).

by the Buddhist practice of viewing the relics in *stupas*. But it was also surely a response to the emphasis on the aspect of god in the flesh ("right before your eyes" [*sakshat*]), with flesh-and-blood qualities (*sa-guna*), in contrast with the aspect of god "without qualities" (*nir-guna*) that the philosophers spoke of.

Artists, both Hindu and Buddhist, have always painted the eyes on a statue last of all, for that is the moment when the image comes to life, when it can *see* you, and you can no longer work on it; that is where the power begins.[4] Rajasthani storytellers who use as their main prop a painting of the epic scenes explained to one anthropologist that once the eyes of the hero were painted in, neither the artist nor the storyteller regarded it as a piece of art: "Instead, it became a mobile temple . . . the spirit of the god was now in residence."[5] The Vedic gods Varuna and Indra were said to be "thousand-eyed," because as kings they had a thousand spies, overseeing justice, and as sky gods they had the stars for their eyes. The sun is also said to be the eye of the sky, and Hindu texts make numerous analogies between human eyes and the sun. Varuna in the *Rig Veda* (2.27.9) is unblinking, a characteristic that later becomes one of the marks that distinguish any gods from mortals.[6] (The texts usually list five ways to recognize a god: gods do not sweat, have dust on them, or cast a shadow; their feet do not quite touch the ground, and they do not blink.)

In the mythology of *darshan*, blinding is generally a bad thing, and sight a good thing. The hagiography of the 8th century Nayanar saint Cuntarar tells us that Shiva blinded him (*darshan* in its negative form) after he deserted his second wife but restored his vision (*darshan* in its positive form) when he returned home to her again. But the theme of the blinded martyr also appears in Hinduism in a significantly altered form: now it is the martyr who blinds himself. This happens in the story of

---

4. Richard F. Gombrich, "The Buddha's Eye, the Evil Eye, and Dr. Ruelius" in Heinz Bechert, ed., *The Dating of the Historical Buddha/Die Datierung des historischen Buddha*. Part 2 (Symposien zur Buddhismusforschung, 4/2; Göttingen: Vandenhoeck & Ruprecht, 1992), 335–38.

5. William Dalrymple, "Homer in India: Rajasthan's Oral Epics" in The *New Yorker*, November 20, 2006, 48–55; here, 52.

6. Wendy Doniger, *Splitting the Difference: Gender and Myth in Ancient Greece and India* (Chicago: The University of Chicago Press, 1999).

the Nayanar saint named Kannappar, told in several texts,[7] perhaps best known from the 12th century Tamil *Periya Purana*:

> Kannappar was the chief of a tribe of dark-skinned, violent hunters, who lived by hunting wild animals (with the help of dogs) and stealing cattle. One day he found Shiva in the jungle; filled with love for the god and pity that he seemed to be all alone, Kannappar resolved to feed him. So he took pieces of the meat of a boar that he had killed, tasted each one to make sure it was tender, and brought the meat to him. He kicked aside, with his foot, the flowers that a Brahmin priest had left on Shiva's head and spat out on him the water from his mouth. Then he gave him the flowers that he had worn on his own head. His feet, and his dogs' paws, left their marks on him. He stayed with him all night, and left at dawn to hunt again. The Brahmin priest, returning there, removed Kannappar's offerings and hid and watched him. In order to demonstrate for the Brahmin the greatness of Kannappar's love, Shiva caused blood to flow from one of his eyes. To staunch the flow, Kannappar gouged out his own eye with an arrow and replaced the god's eye with his. When Shiva made his second eye bleed, Kannappar put his left foot on Shiva's eye to guide his hand, and was about to pluck out his remaining eye when Shiva stretched out his hand to stop him, and placed Kannappar at his right hand.[8]

Kannappar is a tribal beyond the Hindu pale; he does not seem to know the rules of Brahmin *dharma*, such as the taboo on offering flesh to the gods. He does not know about the impurity of substances, like spit, that come from the body—the spit that he uses to clean the image as a mother would use her spit to scrub a bit of dirt off the face of her child. He reverses the proper order of head and foot by putting his foot on the head of the god, instead of his head on the god's foot, the usual gesture of respect.

Kannapar does not understand metaphor: the normal offering to a god is a flower, perhaps a lotus, and in fact he gives the god flowers

---

7. The story is retold in the Sanskrit *Skanda Purana, Kedara Khanda* 5, 111–197 and 22.1–64; see Wendy Doniger, "The Scrapbook of Undeserved Salvation: The *Kedara Khanda* of the *Skanda Purana*" in Wendy Doniger, ed., *Purana Perennis, Purana Perennis: Reciprocity and Transformation in Hindu and Jaina Texts* (Albany: SUNY Press, 1993), 66–70.

8. *Periya Purana* 16 (650–830), pp. 71–86 of *Periya Purana* of Cekkilar., trans. Alistair McGlashan , *The History of the Holy Servants of the Lord Siva* (Victoria, British Columbia: Trafford Publishing, 2006).

(though ones that have been polluted, in high caste terms, by being worn on his own head). But Sanskrit poets often liken beautiful eyes to lotuses, and Kannappar offers the god the real thing, the eye, the wrong half of the metaphor. But his "mistakes" are *felix culpas* that make possible an unprecedentedly direct exchange of gazes: instead of trading mere glances, he and the god trade their very eyes. This is *darshan* in its most direct, violent, passionate form.

Thus the idea of *darshan*, of seeing the god and, more important, of knowing that the god sees you, became central to Hinduism and accounts for the extraordinary emphasis on the eyes in Hindu mythology. But the doctrine of *darshan* is the mirror image of the philosophy of illusion. The concept of *darshan* in these myths reverses the valence of vision/sight/gaze in Indian philosophy, where the eyes lie, and becoming blind to the world is the only way to resist being seduced by god's illusion. It is tempting to see these two bodies of texts as agonistic, responding to one another, but I don't think we can do that. The chronology is not clear enough, nor is there any sense of competition. Rather, I think the texts are aware of one another, particularly because both the doctrine of illusion and the practice of *darshan* are extremely popular and widespread in India.

CONCLUSION

Each approach supplements the other. In the everyday world, vision is a good thing, and the best way to reach god. In the world of meditation and renunciation, which is the world of the philosophy of illusion, vision also functions ultimately as a good thing, though in a more indirect way, a kind of *felix culpa*: by showing us how flawed vision is, and how foolish we are to trust our eyes, it leads us to a more profound distrust of the material world, and turns us away to seek a very different way to reach a very different aspect of god.

Wendy Doniger
Presented at Garrett-Evangelical Theological Seminary
May 1, 2010

PART 3

Arts, Film, and Medicine

7

Light and Life

The Ministry of Vincent Van Gogh

Kenneth Vaux
with Richard Vaux and Jan van Eys

> ... *the real significance of what great artists and serious masters tell us in their masterpieces is that to lead us to God . . . one writes a book, another paints a picture.*[1]

Now the sacrament is not prayer shawl and Torah, font and scripture, prayer rug and Qur'an—but paint and brush. The journey for Vincent involved great pain. His life through dark valleys and brilliant fields bears out Rachmaninoff's dictum, "no suffering, no melody." His heart ached to find ministry, until ministry found him in his artist's satchel.

In those tools, and in God witnessed in nature's scenes, he would capture sermons such as the gnarled "Potato Eaters" and glorious fields of blue "Irises" (from the gardens of his lunatic [moonstruck] asylum in Provence). The parable that arose from his palette was not Michelangelo's idealized realism as in the "Mona Lisa" or in Picasso's fractured cry of agony in "Guernica," but a mingling of respect for "the least of these" and a *chanson* of enduring hope.

Vincent was one of the last men of the age of faith and the first of the age of anxiety. He bore in his body and mind the Lenten admonition:

---

1. Vincent Van Gogh, quoted in Marc Edo Traulbaut, *Vincent Van Gogh* (East Sussex, U.K.: Art Books International, 1981), 71.

"Dust thou art, to dust thou shalt return." Yet he cast his eyes to the sun by day and to the starry, starry night. The ministry of Vincent Van Gogh offers a lens for us to view not only sight and light, but also interfaith theological insight.

Some decades ago, Ken and Sara, along with their friend Jan van Eys, a medical doctor at M.D. Anderson hospital, collaborated at the Institute of Religion in Houston, Texas. At that time, we were involved in the construction of the Rothko Chapel. The Philip Johnson chapel housed the famous murals of Mark Rothko—large panels of deep wine and dioxazine purple, burnt umber, and absorbing black—a foretaste of Rothko's own suicide (1970) and a blood-witness, like that of Vincent, to the deep pieties of faith and justice in an unjust, homicidal, persecutorial, and anguished world.

At the opening of the Rothko Chapel, whose art was torn from the soul of one whose people had become dust at the incinerating hand of a Eucharistic people, a largely Christian congregation joined the sponsoring family of Jean and Dominique de Ménil in a sacramental and Eucharistic contemplation—as if it were being held at Michelangelo's Sistine Chapel in Rome or the Matisse Chapel in Venice. Both sacred places were sanctuary models for the de Ménil's and Rothko's vision. The dark colors of Rothko seemed profound and endless in the subdued lighting of the chapel, offering a deep space for meditation. Barnett Newman's "Broken Obelisk," dedicated to Martin Luther King, Jr., stood in the courtyard. We still remember the dedication as we watched in the courtyard, with an occasional glance to the ramshackle white clapboard house next door. Here, a distraught "tea-partyer" of his day sat in his window holding a rifle, his contorted tribute to Dr. King.

As the worship/dedication concluded, the choir of Houston Baptist University sang another prophetic song of the day, "Bridge Over Troubled Waters." Love is to lay down the bridge of one's life—Vincent and Rothko. The clue to this strange mélange of sadness, service, and salvation is the ministry of Vincent Van Gogh, a ministry of light and life. After some introductory notes, let us explore this ministry in three movements—a triptych:

- Coal-mine ministry and subterranean darkness and madness;
- Slash of ear, splash of color: psychedelics or *Geisteslebens*; and
- Glory and the illumination of the commonplace.

Light and Life 87

INTRODUCTION

As we planned and crafted Project Interfaith and sketched out an inaugural workshop on light and sight, several serendipitous developments cheered our work.

- Ken's still-little brother and close buddy across the years drove out from Long Island—our family home and high school at Sewanhaka. The island also was the sometime home of Rothko and Jackson Pollack. He crossed the glorious Appalachian Mountains to the Pennsylvania cabin that landmarks the long ancestral homestead of the families of both our parents. It was Ken's 70th birthday bash. Having heard of our conceived Project Interfaith and the light/sight inaugural workshop, he offered to exhibit a set of his lightscapes. His latest work—much in the spirit of Russian icons (*e.g.*, Andrei Rublev's "Trinity") and Japanese rock-garden paintings—resonated beautifully with the motifs of the workshop.

  I had already sought out experts on the work of Van Gogh and talked with Harvard philosophy professor Elaine Scarry—whom I had met at 2007 lectures at Cambridge where she spoke on the "philosophy of color" (following her work on "the splendor of the human body"). I was especially moved by her talk on "Green and the Novels of Charles Dickens." Our fellow panelist, Bill Murphy ("Violence and Obscurity: Religious Cosmology of Seeing and Hearing in the West African Rainforest"), also shared with me the work of a University of Chicago physicist who had written on the physics and philosophy of light and color in Monet's series on Rouen Cathedral.

- The thought of Van Gogh—and a several-year research undertaking on Vincent's ministry moment in Petit-Wasmes, Borinage, Belgium, very close to our daughter Sarah's home in Antwerp—led us to explore a course at Yale and an unfinished project offered by Henri Nouwen on the ministry of Vincent Van Gogh. This pioneer pastoral-theologian[2] had often found his way into Sara and Ken's teaching and into Jan's care for children

---

2. See Henri Nouwen, *The Wounded Healer: Ministry in Contemporary Society* (New York: Random House, 1979).

with cancer. We asked ourselves whether our competencies and circumstances—theology, art, film, and ministry plus a permanent free-bed-and-board in Antwerp—might allow us to give continuing life to Father Nouwen's wonderful project. This article will possibly extend into an upcoming sabbatical book on the ministry of Van Gogh, which has been encouraged and assisted by the Henri Nouwen Archives in Toronto. In any case, this was another lens on the Light/Sight endeavor.

DARKNESS IN INTERFAITH PURVIEW

As I write today, Placido Domingo prepares to sing the baritone lead in Verdi's "Simon Boccanegra." Not the *Tenor Ittalien* or *Heldentenor*, not even the conductor, but the baritone! He comments before the performance: "In this dark opera, with many voices of dark color, the only tenor (romantic hero) is a baritone" (the perennial fantasy of tenors).

Last night, the Symphonic Wind Ensemble at Northwestern University considered the subject of darkness in four compositions. Included were Henry Purcell's "Music for the Funeral of Queen Mary" and "*Et exspecto resurrectionem mortuorum*" by Olivier Messiaen. The program notes spoke of Messiaen as "seeing colors internally when hearing sounds" (cf., Torrance's connection between light and word). In the phenomenon known as "synesthesia"—". . . a major chord with an added sixth, for example, was always bright blue—the blue of Chartres, the Mediterranean, heaven" (and eternity— Hegel "*Ewigkeit ist Blau*"). This was the "music of the spheres" that Mozart heard and Vincent saw.

Van Gogh's first sketches in his decade-long career were dark and muddy. We think of "The Sower" and "Evening Prayer" (early 1881). His early works, before the inspiration from the impressionists' color palette, were dark and brooding—emerging from his interest in form and content, but also influenced by the gloom of the coal mines.

This was also the time of his early missionary impulses and experiences. Following his passion to "preach the Gospel everywhere," while he was free-lancing in art dealing in London, he became an assistant to a Methodist minister. Before 1880, he flirted with formal religious ministry. His father and grandfather were Dutch Reformed pastors. He articulated early that his life was about "a knowledge of the one true God," which in good Calvinist tradition was the source of "true knowledge of the self."

(Book I, The Institutes). Again, in the Calvinist tradition of "calling," Vincent was obsessed that his life "have meaning," and that meaning was meant to arise in his work (vocation). [3] After failing in this institutional attempt to serve God (much like my seminarian who, after years of failure as a preacher, discovered that his youthful vision of a cloudscape forming the letters PC meant "plant corn," not "preach Christ"), Vincent found his genuine calling in the ministry of art.

When he returned home from the sojourn in England, he worked in a bookshop in Dordrecht (on the German border). More than selling books, he seemed to be busy translating Bible verses between Dutch, French, and English languages—the *vielsprachig* Dutch, Flemish, and Belgian church-folk have always been ideal Wycliffe translators. He went to Amsterdam to the university to study theology in the Reformed Faculty, but it didn't work. In Ken's view, he was not so much a "learned Calvinist" pastor type, but probably a pastor-missionary, a hands-on person, one for whom ongoing identity was not so much in the realm of ideas but in personal and interpersonal relationships—a light and sight ministry. Color and light would be his books and canvases—his sermons.

He would find out that insight often comes with frustration. At Borinage, he wrote to his brother Theo: "I must continue on the path I have taken. If I do nothing, if I don't study, if I stop searching, then I am lost, in misery . . . What is your final goal? you may ask. That goal is becoming more clear, it will take shape slowly but surely, as the scribble becomes a sketch and the sketch becomes a painting."[4]

After dropping out of school, he did receive an appointment as an evangelist-missionary in a poor, coal-mining region (Petit-Wasmes in the Borinage sector). Identifying with the poor sheep of his flock, he slept on a bed of straw, gave away his food and clothes, and lived in a back room of a bake-shop. It was here that, at times, he was heard sobbing through the entire night. Depression, *Seele Schaden*, artistic passion, dreams, broken dreams—who knows? Church officials saw this as an inexcusable breach of ministerial dignity—"conduct unbecoming a minister of the Gospel," as we rectitude-obsessed Reformed clergy would have it—and sent him packing.

---

3. Evert Uitert and Louis Van Tilborgh, *The Life and Work of Vincent Van Gogh* (New York: Rizzoli, 1990), 15.

4. Ibid., 15.

Vincent's life and direction were about to change. Objecting to the accusation of sickness or madness, Vincent (according to biographer Robert Hughes) was entering the period when he would experience the "height of his powers. . . . He was longing for precision and grace."[5] To our mind, it was here that Vincent was creatively transformed and his destined ministry was about to begin. The "light of life" now illumined his passionate mind and the virtuosity of the Spirit enabled his well-trained artistry. He was now able to see those faces of the poor and to capture their pain and hope for all time to come.

The light of God always shines through the eyes of "the least of these," his children. Vincent was, like his Paris friend Henri Toulouse-Lautrec who saw through to the soul—God in us, in indomitable humanity, in the midst of suffering, in poverty, enduring the disdain and contempt of the world—the dancers, the prostitutes, the grotesques and people of the street. Lautrec's painting of Van Gogh shows him sitting among such street vagrants, an ashen yet resolute man. In the grand tradition of those who came before him, like Rembrandt and Vermeer, Vincent perceived the shadows and the dramatic flashes of illumination and the *visio Dei* within the contrasts. Be it the Christ or the woman at the kitchen table, these mentors of bygone centuries, and now the angular irascible one with the red hair, saw the glory of God shining in the weary, working faces of the poor.

Artists, who use their God-given skills to convey their perceptions of the light of God, are great evangelists each in their own way. Yet, to tell us about their experience and of the truth of their visions, they must perceive the light of God themselves first and let that light permeate their own consciousness, their own souls. It is the creature's lot that humans must use their bodies and senses to perceive the light.[6]

---

5. Robert Hughes, *Nothing If Not Critical* (London: The Harvill Press, 1990), 144.

6. The care artists give their bodies will always color and potentially distort their visions. Vincent was fond of absinthe, the now-banned beverage that was, in his lifetime, a popular drink in café society. The drink has a seductive visual appeal, undoubtedly attractive to a painter. When poured from a bottle, it is a clear, brilliantly green liqueur. However, because of its bitterness, the drink was traditionally diluted with a specified amount of water, poured through a slotted spoon wherein a sugar cube was placed. This dilution changed the appearance of the glass from clear green to a beautiful yellow opalescence. The ritual of presentation of absinthe would be very attractive to Vincent, as it was to many artists; Toulouse-Lautrec was a habitual absinthe drinker also. However, the chemicals in absinthe, especially the terpenoid thujone, wracked the brain, exacted a

When we preach our faith, we preach our revelation. We ought to prepare ourselves to make our vision as pure and unobstructed as we can. Unfortunately, so often our behavior clouds our perceptions. We preach what we heard and not necessarily what the speaker intended. We paint what we see and not always what was created for us to see. Thus, even the greatest saints are also likely to be the greatest sinners, because they claim clarity while they may have fogged their vision by their actions. But precisely that realization makes their works the more powerful because we do not just recognize the light of God, but also realize our humanness by the brilliant imperfections in the artist's sermon.

DARKNESS AS LIGHT

When the earthly light was about to dim in the eyes of Martin Luther King, Jr. as he stood with the garbage workers in Memphis, he carried a scrap of paper with words of Gandhi and then his own:

> In the midst of death, life persists. In the midst of untruth, truth persists. In the midst of darkness, light persists.
> (Mahatma Gandhi—after Christian and Muslim scripture)
>
> In the midst of darkness and death, whatever happens, give us faith to know that in God we are in light and life
> (Martin Luther King, Jr.)

Gandhi and King, Vincent and Rothko, knew this mystery of crucifixion—that darkness is light. Truth in interfaith purview—i.e., Jesus' faith hallowed by its Judaic and Islamic precedence and resonance—was spoken of by Dominique de Ménil as she dedicated the Rothko Chapel. Her message was Blaise Pascal's sheer word—a Jansenist *Logos*: "We are cluttered with images and only abstract art" (not Mel Gibson's "Passion of the Christ") "can bring us to the threshold of the divine." Hebraic, Christic, and Islamic theology of light teaches us that images often obstruct rather than transfigure. Dignified mute icons may be the only kind of beauty that can convey light and word today. We thank Richard Vaux's iconoclastic icons—his "lightscapes"—for lightening and redeeming our dumpster of poor words of this Light and Sight symposium. Our only

---

price, and shortened the life of the user. Because the mental distortions and convulsions from the terpenes can be alleviated with bromides and aggravated with nicotine use, Vincent was treated with bromides and cutting down on smoking during his institutionalization at Arles.

retort is that of Vincent: words, for those who not only see but read reality (thank you, Jacques Derrida), are the canvases of scripture, Shakespeare, Milton, and all masters of all cultures.

This is why, for the mystic in all traditions—Kabal, Hildegard, Julian, Teresa, Sufi—darkness is light. *Via negativa* is the way to go into light and truth.

The interfaith theological progression of premises goes something like this:

- The truth and light Vincent saw, the dark world could not bear ("not comprehend"/"we hid our faces" (Isa 53).
- The light John the Apostle and Seer saw "shone in the darkness and the darkness could not put it out" (ch. 1).
- The Word that was God—eternal light, eternal Torah (Philo)—was life.
- Allah is the light of heaven and earth (Sura 24).
- In that light, *Logos* was the life of all people.
- Glimpsing that light, we see that all are the children of God.
- We know that light—*Logos, Nor (Siraj)* is *eskanosen*—encamped next to us in the neighbor, the other—*Autre* is *Autrui* (Levinas).
- Light is reflected from THE LIGHT—which is reflected in the face of the other.

SLASH/SPLASH

The second movement in the ministry of Vincent Van Gogh has to do with wound and healing and with Father Henri Nouwen's sublime oxymoron—"the wounded healer." Our global world today is the heir of two "enlightenments"—those associated with the names of Kant and Wesley. These broad phenomena, one worldly, one religious, have been called illuminations and awakenings—*Aufklarung* and *Recussitacion*. How Euro-American culture extends to Africa, Asia, and indigenous America is an issue as replete with controversy as is the connection of Van Gogh with his neighbor King Leopold (Belgian Congo), the gruesome "hand harvester" who came onto the world scene just a few years after the death of Vincent.

Both enlightenments refer to the blind seeing the light and the dead rising to new life—wounds and healing. Theologically, these historical moments are recapitulations of the profound spiritual/physical renaissance (a word embracing both awakening and arising), which is the scriptural charter of healing and the healer, present in all faiths.

Judaism first portrays this matrix of efficacy into the world as a universal phenomenon—a radiation of the One God into this One *oikumene*— one inhabited world. "Your descendents will be as the stars of the sky . . ." (Gen 22:11). Ironically, this passage is also that of the expulsion of Hagar and Ishmael and the double threatened sacrifice of the "beloved son." We learn about this complicated metaphor from Jon Levenson and his set of books on the resurrection.[7] Judaism inherits this matrix of divine power in the world from all primordial faith and ethics—especially from India, Egypt, and Persia. Its essence goes like this—the God of light is the God of life. This divine indicative grounds all human imperative: Heal the sick, forgive sins, teach children, give sight to the blind, house the homeless, let the lame walk, liberate the oppressed, lift the poor, forgive sins, provide work to the unemployed, raise the dead, etc. There you have it—with myriad other interstitial ministries. The purpose of each human life is to reflect out into the world—onto fellow humanity—the light/gift/energy/ *imago*/ that is in us, so that others receive glory and radiate that back on the Creator: "Let your light so shine that humans may see your 'good works' (*Kala erga*) and glorify your Father in heaven" (Matt 5:16).

In this mission, there is no place for colonial condescension or Eurocentric arrogance toward the "benighted souls" of another culture. That would be as dangerous an arrogation in this symposium as the denial that the blind possess their own special light and gift.

Interfaith ethics are all rooted in eternal and temporal Torah. This is the canvas, the tableau of all godliness and goodness. Torah (Law of Christ, *Taurut*) is revealed, then enunciated in prophesy and elucidated in Wisdom. It is the divine depiction (and human discovery) of the rule of faith and life—of "all righteousness" (Rom 8:4).

For Vincent, although he saw this serene picture of the mountain sermon—Sinai rehearsed—his life-pain, perhaps because of an overly severe childhood and disappointing young adulthood, would persist.[8] Just

---

7. See Jon D. Levenson, *The Death and Resurrection of the Beloved Son* (New Haven, Conn.: Yale University Press, 1993).

8. There was clearly an underlying hereditary disease in the Van Gogh family. The

as God is unknowable, and light inaccessible—for now, the light would remain opaque—dim as in a mirror (1 Cor 13:12). Like Count Tolstoy—who tried to actualize the Sermon on the Mount with its perfections on his Russian Estate—that estate would crumble—and Vincent would take his ear and then his life.

Yet he had seen the mountaintop. He emerged from the mud and dirt, from the "Bearers of the Burden," the hard, bent-down miners carrying out the bags of coal (1881); he left the Berinage and ended up in Brussels. Now in the world of *apperception Français*, he dreamed of *le pays des tableaux*—an envisioned canvas of beauty and color—the realm of imagination and possibility, the good world and the goodness of life, the domain of the poet and artist—the splash of color—as Jackson Pollack might dream, then toss. This possible, ideal realm slowly came into Vincent's view. This was the earthly paradise—the Kindom (*sic*) come on earth—Rousseau's "The Peaceable Kingdom." Like Bach, he could almost see and touch it—yet not quite (see Hindemith's study of Bach). *Ad majorem Dei gloriam* was possible, but not human apotheosis.

He threw himself into the role of novice artist, went to art school and began the tedious discipline of seeing acutely, perhaps for the first time. The pointillism of human and animal anatomy, and the free yet mimetic technique of drawing, then coloring, became his gift. He was now noticing the "Other." He was witnessing a solidarity with the creation, the whole human family—especially the weak and hurting. Such service he discovered would require discipline and sacrifice. He was discovering what the Sermon on the Mount portrays as discipleship. In his study of the *Bergpredigt* –The Cost of Discipleship (*Nachfolger*) (1937), Dietrich Bonhoeffer writes "when Christ calls a person he bids him come and die." Rabbinic formation is fine-grained, highly textured believing and action. It is "denying oneself" (first commandment) and, in the Jesus movement, it becomes following in the way of the cross. Vincent's cruciformed life now turned its gaze on the "least of these," his kinsfolk. "Blessed are those who are persecuted for righteousness sake—for theirs is the Kingdom of Heaven" (Matt 5:10).

---

disease that best fits all symptoms, including intermittent mental illness, is acute intermittent porphyria (AIP). AIP and a similar disease, porphyria variegate, were found in the Netherlands. See Wilfred Niels Arnold, *Vincent Van Gogh: Chemicals, Crises, and Creativity* (Boston: Birkhäuser, 1992) and Geoffrey Dean, *The Porphyrias*, 2nd edition (Philadelphia: J.B. Lippincott, 1971).

"The Bearers of the Burden" (1881) was actually completed after a move to Brussels. The missionary remained itinerant—with nowhere to lay his head. In the ancient great city of *Gaul Nord,* he undertook arduous studies in sketching, modeling, and drafting. The letters also suggest that Vincent is undergoing a transition in his understanding of theology and ministry—toward greater realism about himself and those people who would constitute his congregation. Though he wanted to present many sermons (canvases), he knew it was best "to do what was possible" and concentrate on what would be enduring—quality rather than quantity.

He was moving from a hands-on, evangelical ministry to one at large where he hopes to reach greater "humanity" (*anthropon*). Our suspicion is that a cardinal scripture of Reformed Faith—Matthew 5:19—takes on prominence in the mind and heart of Vincent. His vocation to "preach the Gospel" and "make disciples of all nations" (Matt 28) is now more the Sermon on the Mount:

> Let your Light shine . . . That *anthropon* will see your good works (*oeuvre*) . . .
>
> and reflect back glory on your Father, who is in heaven.

Evangelism (as his preceding Bible translation) has now mutated into publication. It is plausible that Vincent knew and loved (at least from his Methodist stint) the well known Reformed hymn, "O Zion haste:"[9] ". . . Publish glad tidings, tidings of peace, tidings of Jesus—redemption and release."

At last, his calling into evangelical ministry was being realized. He left his formal academic studies to study *Dame Nature*—trees and fields, flowers and skies. His virtuosity was validated by his discovery in the early 1880s that watercolors were facile in the depiction of seas and skies.[10] As his work took on the dimension of holistic witness, he became one of

---

9. "O Zion Haste," words by Mary Thompson (1868, 1871); music by James Walch (1875), http://www.cyberhymnal.org.

10. The impressionist palette deals with light—the visible spectrum of red, orange, yellow, green, blue, indigo, violet. To the impressionist, blacks, browns, and grays are achieved by mixing warm and cool colors. Every color has hue (warm or cool or in between), tone or value (lightness to darkness), and intensity (brightness to dullness). The black and umber pigments are considered dark, dull colors—used often to subdue or dull other colors. Van Gogh's umbers were used this way in "The Potato Eaters." When the impressionist idea of painting light inspired Vincent, he began to use cool shadows in warm light ("The Hay Fields") and warm shadows in cool light ("Starry Night.")

the great artists of history—like Michelangelo and Mozart—who might be called evangelical or prophetic artists. "Good works," in the sense of Matthew 5:19, mingled Torah with the sense of task *(aufgabe)* and grace, Gospel, gift *(gabe)*.

"Graceful work" is the insight of Jesus' Sermon on the Mount; the Letter of James, Jesus' brother; the enigmatic ,ephemeral epiphenomenon of Jewish Christianity (which goes into underground Diaspora after the Roman Judao-Christianicide beginning in 66 c.e.); and this mood also gave rise to the syneidesis and the Islamic conjunction of *Taurut* and *Injil* (law and gospel). This elusive faith tradition is the gift to humanity of interfaith wisdom . . . that humanity may see your good works (faith-prompted *oeuvre*) and glorify your Father in heaven.

Faith and life, animated in the Torah-Spirit legacy of Pentecost, a recapitulation of Creation, where the Holy Spirit superintended the "Days of Creation"—is at work in the pain and passion that Vincent entered in 1880. In his stumbling way, he spoke of an overarching totality of his *oeuvre*—greater than any particular work. "What I am trying to do," he wrote in 1888 shortly before his death, "is to succeed in creating a coherent whole."[11]

ANTWERP

Before the final moments of sacrifice and glory in Provence, severe chastening, maddening and trying years of vocational maturation occur in The Hague, in the parental parsonage of Neunen, culminating in decisive years in Antwerp and Paris.

The magnificent steeple of the Cathedral in Antwerp and the breathtaking Rubens Christ oils –nativity, life scenes, crucifixion, and resurrection—captivated Vincent's imagination. To these, he added the museums, dock landings, landscapes, townscapes, seascapes, skyscapes—the vitalities of this vibrant city—which he found dramatic in their valences of light and color. Ultimate intrigue was found nevertheless—in the faces of people, especially the peasants and workers. Persons' bodies irradiated with the stigmata of smallpox and the beautiful heads of women in the Scala Café again, illumined by the stunning lightscapes—even at dusk and dark—riveted his imagination, his spectacular delight and his deep sympathy and compassion.

11. Van Tilborgh, 16.

At this point, we might mention the series of Vincent's *Leben Jesus* works, some of which may take their inspiration from this pilgrimage in Antwerp. "The Raising of Lazarus," an intriguing sower with a Jesus head and a bandage wrapping the ears (which some have called "Jesus Van Gogh"), "The Good Samaritan," and "Pieta"—all marked by that tell-tale swath of sandy, red hair—suggest a Christocentric concentration of being, which Vincent and many before and after have experienced in the sacred spaces of the great Antwerp churches.

In Antwerp, fellow artists rejected his unrefined and bold style of sketching. The few models available rebuffed his crudity and scorned his candid portrayals. Soon, he packed his saddle-bags and headed for *la Belle Paris* which—with its cache of artists and critics, along with her distant suburbs in Provence—would be his Jerusalem.

PARIS AND PROVENCE—THE DENOUEMENT

His face was turned to his destiny and there was no turning back. He was now the people's painter, and the priests and publicans would not put up with it. He would challenge the canons of art and the protocols and provenance of the artist. He knew Paris as the art capital of the world from his work in the world of art-business. In Paris, he loved Montmartre and hung out with Lautrec. He also exhibited with Seurat, Delacroix, Signac, Gauguin, and Pissarro. He planned to work at Cormon's studio drawing nude and classical models. This proved to be redundant and too expensive, but a season of immense value. In a poor man's diversion, he did red poppies, blue corn flowers, white and rose roses, and yellow chrysanthemums—trying to reconcile *les tons rompus et neutres*—intense and muted lights and colors. He was a reluctant adventurer, having become "a stranger in his own home and family," thus exemplifying another characteristic of early Christian ministry.

Since he viewed Delacroix's 1850 work, "Christ on the Lake of Gennesaret," in Paris, it was only a matter of time until Vincent would seek the calming of the waters of his troubled mind by the master's words, "peace, be still." He was now ready to venture into the Mediterranean waters of southern France, finally to execute his own "Fishing Boats at Sea" in 1888. His closing days in Provence were still marked by interpersonal and professional conflict, by advancing mental illness, by a serene recognition of his own gifts, his limitations, and his mortality. Still this time is marked by a phenomenal flash and splash of light and color that still brings ecstasy and wonder to the world 100 years later.

He rented four rooms in the Yellow House and assembled an impressive set of paintings to send to Theo a portfolio, which would add to the serious formation of a *Gesammelte Werke,* which we now measure as nearly 1000 paintings and a similar number of drawings. Vincent's goal of a coherent body of work that would present a witness to the world—a witness both esthetic and theistic—was taking shape though, like other persons of genius—da Vinci and Michelangelo, Mozart, Schubert, and Beethoven—he never imagined or dreamed that such global reception was already underway.

The argument with Gauguin continued the Parisian critique, not only of the classical school but also of the impressionist and neo-impressionist movements of art. Vincent had been thriving as the summer light, color, and warmth took hold. "The Green Vineyard," "The Night Café," two "Night Scenes," "The Café Terrace," "Starry Night," "Bedroom in Arles" (Ken Vaux's favorite, which he has had had on his wall for 60 years) and the compositions of "The Trinquetaille Bridge" formed a colorful autumnal portfolio. By Christmas, the volatile tempers of Gauguin and Van Gogh had exploded, Vincent mutilated his ear, and he was admitted to the hospital in Arles.

The Christmas-eve mutilation surely came from a combination of his frustration and illness and mounting disdain and criticism. His neighbors objected to him living in the yellow house—a ne'er-do-well and consorter with the derelict and sinners. No, Methodist, puritan disciplines were not for him. Drink and prostitutes were his fare, and even his "Skull of a Skeleton with Burning Cigarette" (1885) sported the burning butt of a cigarette. Yet, grace abounded with every sin.

In the asylum at St. Remy, he began his series on irises and lilacs. His garden with pine trees reminds Ken of the woodlands garden south of his study with hemlocks, blue and green spruce, and a long-needle pine—evergreen tributes to friends for whom he has had the honor of offering the services of death and resurrection. Later, he would sketch and paint the enclosed fields and other Provencal montages. Finally, toward the end of his days, we receive the pre-Dali-esque church and houses at *Auvers.* For Ken, the scene is already Passover *Kadosh*—a scene of holy sacrifice. At the hospital at Arles, he meditated among the Moorish arches and pools reminiscent of the *Mesquite* at Cordova. The watercolors of budding peach trees portend the new life of his yearning and dreams.

PHYSICIAN, HEAL THYSELF

When Paul Tillich was university professor at Chicago, he would consort with we who were his students at Jimmy's Tavern on 55th Street and Woodlawn. One could feel here the flickering twilight companionship of the Vincents of this world. When Tillich gave the graduation address to our class at Princeton Seminary, he introduced what would become a famous sermon: "Heal the sick—Cast out Demons." He posed the proleptic faith and hope of Vincent's tattered life and *oeuvre*. How poignant and powerful it is when Jesus' inaugural witness pertains also to himself—"I come to bring sight to the blind, good news to the poor, release to the captives and new life to the dying" (Luke 4). Vincent's intriguing physician in his last days—Doctor Gachet—could watch his patient ebbing, as new life was breaking out in and through him. Together, they walked out and made sketches, even as *dénouement* loomed.

Paradoxical mystery abounds as we contemplate the ministry of Vincent Van Gogh. We can only ask, "Can madness actually be sanity, schizoid insight, actually truth—foolishness, wisdom, suffering, health—death life?" In the words of the song, "Starry, Starry Night," "they would not listen, they did not know how—perhaps they never will."

With the 20/20 vision of hindsight, we can see that Vincent's body and mind were disintegrating, even as his gift to the world was dramatically being born. Again, we are dealing with the biblical miracles: "He must increase while I must decrease" and "who saves his life will lose it and who loses his life for my sake –will find it" (John 3:30, Mark 8: 35).

When he painted "Still Life with Open Bible" (1885), with the Bible opened to Isaiah 53, "the suffering servant," he likely made reference to his Christology and his own biography. To compound the mystery, he placed alongside on the table Zola's *La Joie de Vivre*. The text of Isaiah speaks volumes, ". . . He was wounded for our iniquity . . . He is despised and rejected by men, a man of sorrows and acquainted with grief" and " He shall see his seed, be satisfied and prolong his days, . . . I will divide him a portion with the great." It seems that we are dealing with the paradoxical biblical miracles: "He must increase, while I must decrease" and "who saves his life will lose it and who loses his life for my sake will find it" (John 3:30, Mark 8: 35). Vincent once confessed to Theo that, although he didn't have children himself, his works—and (those born to light and life by the viewing)—were his children.

CONCLUSION

The reader may object that, in reflecting on a sublime theme like "the light of the world," we are confusing a secular phenomenon with a sacred process. The validity of that comment must be determined by examining the nature of what is called "the light of the world." In this symposium, we have explored extents, lineaments, and characteristics of that reality—scientific and metaphysical, secular and sacred, even physical and spiritual. Through the interfaith lens, we see that the "light of the world" refers to the Christ, to Word and Truth, to the radiation of God into the world and the reflection of humankind back to the light-source of all creation.

It also refers to the very secular vision of experienced light and color in the realm of human sight. We embrace a vast array of metaphoric meanings. If this breadth and range of meanings are valid, we have made the case that the ministry of Vincent Van Gogh participates in the "light of the world"—which is ministry in the life of God.

Van Gogh and Gauchet were fellow travelers in the parable of light and darkness, life and death, salvation and damnation. "He's sicker than I am," quipped Vincent, deluding himself that he was the sane savior and Gauchet the pathetic patient—and this is how he would picture him. As they made rendezvous near the Auvers Church, his precise line already showed a Dali-esque bent. The journey was already one of salvation and damnation. In the spring sun of Arles and the warmth of August at Auvers (1890), if he knew the hymn, as he most likely did from his Methodist time in England, the pastor would have hummed the hymn of glory:

> In the cross of Christ I glory,
> Towering o'er the wrecks of time;
> All the Light of sacred story
> Gathers round its head sublime.
> When the woes of life o'ertake me,
> Hopes deceive and fears annoy,
> Never shall the cross forsake me
>
> Lo! it glows with peace and joy.
> When the sun of bliss is beaming,

Light and Love upon my way,
From the cross the radiance streaming,
Adds more luster to the day.
Bane and blessing, pain and pleasure,
By the cross are sanctified;
Peace is there that knows no measure,
Joy that through all time abide.[12]

Vincent, with his blended or confused Arminian and Calvinist heritage, his tension of humanist and theist values, his oscillation between health and illness, now faced his future and destiny with faith and foreboding. He was secure in his savior, in the words of the Calvinist Heidelberg Catechism—'his only hope in life and death'—yet uncertain at the fate of his bodily and mental existence. In all, in the midst of death, he could begin to feel the possibility of an immortality rising from the gift of divine strength in his works. So, with the apostle, he was now ready "to work out his salvation with fear and trembling," knowing that it was God working within "to will and do His good pleasure." (Phil 2.12–13)

To his worldly-dimming and now heavenly-clearing eyes, he seemed to see only white fields outside the confining walls. In these remarkable compositions ("Wheat Field with Cypresses," 1889), through the eyes of faith, we might envision those redemptive/evangel fields of that Galilean peasant preacher, perhaps looking out on crowds with their sun-drenched, Palestine headwear: "look on the fields, they are already ripe unto harvest" (John 4:35).

Kenneth Vaux, Richard Vaux, and Jan van Eys
April 2010

---

12. John Bowring (lyrics, 1825); Rathbun (music, 1849), "In the Cross of Christ I Glory," http://www.cyberhymnal.org/htm/i/n/intcross.htm.

8

Light and Sight in Clint Eastwood's *Gran Torino*

Sara Anson Vaux

YOU MAY HAVE HEARD of *Gran Torino*. It's that movie everyone was waiting for: *Dirty Harry* Number Six. For months I waited, enthralled by the trailer that played for months before its December 2008 opening. I guess Eastwood had to make another Dirty Harry revenge movie. He has so many children to support, and Dirty Harry sells big.

EASTWOOD IN A NEW LIGHT

But what a pity! Eastwood spent the past 30 years acting in and sometimes directing movies with lots of audience appeal, like all five Dirty Harry movies[1] and *Every Which Way But Loose* (1978). He alternated the big movies with "personal" but little-seen movies that he directed and funded himself like *Bronco Billy* (1980) and *Honkytonk Man* (1982). *The Outlaw Josey Wales* in 1976 and *Bridges of Madison County* in 1995 had a little more traction, in part because he still was the number-one actor in the world. But he didn't begin to get major director's press until *Unforgiven* in 1992 and *Mystic River* in 2003. Since then it's been one brilliant movie after another, including *Changeling* last year, with Angelina Jolie. So why, I asked myself, was he doing another Dirty Harry?

Not that The Man With No Name, Dirty Harry, The Stranger from *High Plains Drifter*, and the Preacher from *Pale Rider* have gone away, replaced by the soft, gentle, and sympathetic Robert Kinkaid from *Bridges*

---

1. *Dirty Harry* (Don Siegel, 1971); *Magnum Force* (Ted Post, 1973); *The Enforcer* (James Fargo, 1976); *Sudden Impact* (Clint Eastwood, 1983); *The Dead Pool* (Buddy Van Horn, 1988).

of *Madison County* and vulnerable and affectionate Frankie Dunn from *Million Dollar Baby*. The lone and unhappy heroes are still all there in *Gran Torino*'s first half, like a good old buddy, all wrapped up in the figure of Walt Kowalski, the movie's central character. As film critic Manohla Dargis has written, "Dirty Harry is back, in a way, in Gran Torino, not as a character but as a ghostly presence. He hovers in the film, in its themes and high-caliber imagery, and of course most obviously in Mr. Eastwood's face."[2]

The mythic apparatus of the Superhero is present, too, in Walt's acid one-liners and in the giant rifle he packs not too far out of reach. In real life, the one man American superhero model hasn't worked out too well: look at Iraq and Afghanistan. But vigilante justice, so hot a topic in some circles in 2010, particularly in the Southwest? What was a philosopher like Eastwood doing with the wild-cannon vigilante response in such troubled times? And if he presents violence to reject it (as he did in *Unforgiven*), how would he neutralize its seductive on-screen appeal?

GRAN TORINO AND VIOLENCE AND FORGIVENESS

I'll preempt the rest of the paper by saying that he does it in part with the canny use of light—and an array of visual, spatial, and sonic devices that trigger all the senses. Light, darkness, and shadow have enriched Eastwood's compositional palette since his earliest days as a filmmaker, the legacy of his shrewd mentors, Sergio Leone (the Spaghetti westerns) and Don Siegel (*Dirty Harry; Escape from Alcatraz*) and the creative gifts of three talented cinematographers, Bruce Surtees, Jack Green, and now Tom Stern. That may be more information than you want to know, but then with a team-oriented player like Eastwood, we can't ignore the emotional power of the various cinematic tools that help tell the story he has in mind. And that story is a shocking one for audiences that recently have been subjected to an astounding amount of hate speech about immigrants, Blacks, and "foreigners"—to wit, other human beings. Violence, as Nelson Mandela always said, is not the way. But what is? *Gran Torino* posits some answers.

Let me give you a quick summary of *Gran Torino*'s plot. The "story world" is set in a formerly booming, now rundown, American industrial

---

2. "Hope for a Racist, and Maybe a Country," *The New York Times* (Friday, December 12, 2008), C1.

city, Detroit, with its formerly all-white pristine neighborhoods overtaken by waves of immigrants. The protagonist, Walt, embodies the dreams of a better life of one early immigrant strand, the Polish. For his whole life, he worked on a Ford assembly line and took pride in his craft and his tidy home. He is now retired. Blacks, Hispanics, and Asians have drifted into his neighborhood, and now, heaven forfend, an extended Hmong family has moved in next door.

In this painfully timely movie, Eastwood links depression and spiritual uncertainty to a past history of violent acts, associating markers of personal disintegration with larger economic and social instability indirectly or directly caused by war. Sequence after sequence, Eastwood unspools spiritual and social dislocation: Walt and the war memories that poison his life; his alienation from his children; the collapsing city within which he lives; and the difficulty with fashioning a human community that embraces rather than rejects difference. The categories into which Walt files people—the ethnic slurs he spits out nonstop—have become structures of exclusion for him and barriers to growth for the country around him.

Gran Torino opens with alienating devices that anticipate its later exposure of buried secrets. A long god's-eye sweep of the camera alights upon a modest church building surrounded by grass and cement. The camera dips inside to investigate the building's interior, where a massive organ fills the sanctuary with solemn music. It's a funeral, but for whom? The roving camera moves in slowly on a tall, gaunt man who stands beside a coffin, his face barely lit, a poor creature whom the camera isolates as it begins to rove around the gaping spaces trying to catch a snarl here, a yawn there, or a few words of irreverence or kindness. The funeral might as well be for him.

With economical whispered dialogue, we learn that the funeral is for the man's wife, yet we hear his sons scorn him and his grandchildren admit that they feel no sense of gravity or loss at their grandmother's death. One friend, Al, comes forward to console Walt, for that is his name. Otherwise, he stands alone in cold darkness, comfortless. Rather than the classic organ background that plays at the funeral, the film could have opened with "I'll Walk Alone," the wrenching period song that underscores the beginning of Eastwood's problematic, sad antiwar movie of 2006, *Flags of our Fathers*. Isolation is established visually and thematically as surely here as in the beginning of *Flags of Our Fathers*, where a young soldier stares desperately around him, unmoored in a grey and pitted battlefield.

Funeral Scene in Church and Funeral "Meal" at Walt's House

Revealed in quick snapshots at the church and afterwards during the meal, Walt's jerky sons and smart-mouthed grandchildren inhabit the world of *commedia dell'Arte*, fools (the "Zanni") galore. They seem to be playing in a different movie from the ones we've expected from Eastwood since *Unforgiven, Mystic River,* and *Million Dollar Baby*.3 They are completely cut off from Walt's life—his illness, loneliness, and approaching death—and have no sense of the political and social crises that exist all around them.

Gran Torino as a film, and Walt as a highly sentient character, are acutely aware of both—the ravages of mortality and the savage, multi-layered disintegration of a great urban environment. Eastwood has dealt with these themes from multiple historical perspectives before, but nowhere except in *Unforgiven* has he dug so deeply into a single person's felt culpability for the world within which he lives and has helped, even unknowingly, to create.

"Unforgiven" as a movie title, moreover, laid on top of a nesting doll of manufactured narratives about real and supposed murders, ends in its bookended scrolled test (the final layer of conjectures and possible lies) with the conflicted protagonist's supposed success in "dry goods." The murders we think we witnessed—Davey's, anguished and drawn out—or those of the men in the saloon, distanced by the movie's surreal leap into visual mythologizing—are neither "deserved" nor "forgiven," to assume theological judgment in a film that questions whether such terms bear any meaning at all.

Gran Torino revisits the emotional and theological territory of guilt and forgiveness much more openly than *Unforgiven* does, despite (or perhaps in part because of) the formal and thematic perfection of the earlier movie. *Gran Torino*, like *Flags of Our Fathers, Mystic River,* and *Bridges of Madison County* among other Eastwood films, posits the existence of an earlier "fault" (or at least a deeply buried secret) that must be unearthed,

---

3. Note, though, that *Bridges of Madison County* and *A Perfect World* also contain such characters—the clueless children of Francesca (Meryl Streep), for instance, and the bumbling law officers in *World* (one played by Eastwood himself). The alternate narrative worlds are discussed by Kent Jones in *Physical Evidence* (2008).

acknowledged, and "confessed" for the narrative to move forward. The stain, in Paul Ricoeur's terms, must be cleansed.

We are never completely sure that the "crimes" in Will Munny's past actually occurred, or if they did, were they excused by the massive fraternal slaughter of the Civil War, which unleashed at least a decade of unchecked violence by men unhinged by the war years? The evidence in *Bridges* (the Journal) and *Flags* (the photo; the war medal) is hidden in trunks; the tumultuous reality of the characters' dilemmas is emotionally filtered by extended flashbacks. The revolver in *Mystic River* is hidden in an attic, with almost no one in the movie except detective Sean Devine (Kevin Bacon) ever aware of its cosmic as well as personal significance in the movie's poisoned atmosphere.

HEALING AND VIGILANTE JUSTICE

In *Gran Torino*, Walt Kowalski also has a trunk with a photo and a war medal, hidden in his basement and seen perhaps for the first time (significantly, in almost total darkness) by his grandchildren. The secrets the trunk hides have been festering in his heart for fifty years, to be revealed in spurts throughout the film but never fully understood until the end despite the repeated attempts of the young parish priest to get Walt to "confess," as his wife wished. The entire film is driven by Walt's attempts to regain the control over his life and destiny that seems to have been lost sometime in his past. He hates immigrants, dirt, shoddy workmanship, laziness, and the world in general. The disaster of the funeral meal is followed by a series of assaults: the messy, noisy "Chinks" next door; the gangs that cruise around the neighborhood; the near-theft of his Gran Torino; the gang attack on his neighbors that he thwarts thanks to his fearsome size, his rifle, and some powerful horror-film lighting. It's just one darn thing after another: Walt against chaos.

Just as we're aching with laughter at the growls and snarls and squints and snappy one-liners like "Get off my lawn" that season Walt's days, and just as we are really, really embarrassed by our own enjoyment, the movie begins to leave its playacting (Walt's cocked finger; the gang members' empty threats) and the comic sheen that derives from our memories of Eastwood and that Magnum .44. It gets more serious in each of its parallel narratives. The gangs' phony posturing with their oversized guns becomes real violence by stages; drumbeats signal Walt's return to the "kill" mode of his wartime past as he first protects his own property then begins to protect his new neighbors' persons. But the alternate narrative begins almost immediately, with Walt's instinctive response to the gang intrusion on the Hmong next door. In the antiphonal structure of this movie, that's the call which will find "response" from the grateful neighbors: food and flowers, which he soundly rejects. But the rejection (of gifts; of friendship) will turn around soon enough.

For healing, not vigilante justice, is on Eastwood's mind in *Gran Torino*. Walt opens his newspaper and a revolutionary horoscope leaps out at him. "You will be given a new chance." So will viewers, even if they initially think the movie endorses the exclusionary hatreds that seem to swirl all around this troubled neighborhood.

Or if they carefully watch the way Eastwood and his cinematographer set up the robbery scene. That's the worst, right? A foreigner breaks into your garage to steal your car—not any car, but a car you helped craft yourself in Detroit's and America's automotive heyday. You dash to your kitchen gun chest, pull out the rifle that stands for American heroism against the enemy, and you shoot the intruder, right? The drumbeats on the soundtrack (which also pulsed under the menu image that displayed Walt's hard-edged profile) get your heart beating fast.

Theft Scene

Walt hears a sound. He looks out his back window and sees light in his back yard (probably flooding the area from a suspended helium lighting apparatus). The outside light creates a mirror reflection of his face in his window, gazing out in anger—an image that will be "answered" in the antiphonal rhythm of this movie before too long to different effect. He bursts into the garage to the accompaniment of loud drumbeats, gun cocked and ready. In a flash of spotlight, we see the robber: Thao, the unhappy teen next door. Too late. The kid, already berated by his family and the local gang as weak and powerless, is dead.

But Eastwood the director literally trips up this vengeance script. Walt and the rifle go flying. The overhead light swings wildly through the partial darkness, fragmenting Walt's figure with every swoop of the fixture and every cut of the camera. Drumbeats and fractured lighting—empty darkness and shadow with targeted edge-lights—will appear throughout the rest of the movie. This is the moment when Walt's hidden past and present anger are countered by an alternative narrative that begins to form: one of warm light, ambient sounds, lush gardens, good-natured banter, comforting darkness, new human connections, and lots of tasty-looking food.

Not only does is the movie divided into two halves, question and response, but its expansive structure allows the second narrative to run parallel to the first, soon to overtake it.

Sue, daughter of the Hmong family next door, invades his space and his life, beckoning him toward the wider human family. She insists her brother apologize for the attempted theft and work off his debt. She keeps the banter with Walt going, refusing to accept his sullen dismissal of the rest of the world. Walt rescues her and her distressingly clueless boyfriend Trey (played by Eastwood's son when they wander into a nearby "no-fly" zone (another of those "why don't you people stay in your own neighborhood" kind of places). Returning Sue safely home, the connection between them begins: an open and comic exchange of cultural information about the "Hmong" and gender fault lines; an appeal to be friends.

It isn't long afterwards that we are hysterically and yet (for those of us of a certain age) frighteningly exposed to Walt's extreme vulnerability when one of Walt's ungrateful sons and his wife visit him on his birthday.

Birthday Cake Episode

Unlike the warm light that infused the cab of Walt's pickup when he and Sue conversed about the Hmongs' origins and life in America, and unlike the unsettling hard-lit edges of Walt's figure when he chased the gang members off his lawn, the birthday cake scene with its full-throttled, harsh white light both distorts the space in Walt's dining room and spreads an unhealthy pallor over the wife, the son, and the birthday cake, lying inert on the table like a plastic prop. Even the furniture is distorted: pulled close in toward the figures, flattening the images and crowding the frame. The wife's black and white costume further distorts her features into a mask spouting empty phrases more appropriate to Beckett than to a comforting conversation with an aging family member. Walt pitches them out.

The comic intruders dispatched, the birth date not yet over, we see Walt on his porch with his old dog, looking at his wife's photo, saying, "We sure miss Mama, don't we, Daisy?" This movie can't end well despite the happy connection with Sue only a few scenes earlier. The last time we saw an Eastwood character look at a photo of his dead wife was 1992, when Will Munny began to prepare his tired old body for a bounty hunt that got really, really out of control.

It's time for a change. And here comes Sue with another dinner invitation. Her party has beer; he has cut all the way through his stash. There he goes off his lawn and onto hers, into the crowded house and toward a new life.

LIGHT AND SOUND

The transition from part one to part two of the movie, the *peripeteia* in the plot and the *metanoia* in Walt's spiritual journey, is effected tidily by Eastwood's and Stern's use of sound and light, *son et lumière*, as in a European cathedral. The movie in general is antiphonal and moody, like a religious ritual, which makes the use of light even more critical; light helps interpret the story and signal shifts in the narrative.

In movies as in the theatre, the position and placement of the lights, their number—one, three, or more—and nature—a single light source or a helium balloon—alters the "temperature" of a shot or scene. What direction is the light coming from? What's the motivation of the light: to induce fear, comfort, bring a background into focus or obscure objects? To glamorize or thicken a face of figure and why? Eastwood, as we've seen, uses a lot of edge lighting: why effect does it have? Think candles vs. florescent lights in a church. Think natural light vs. a whole lighting setup, like the Northwestern University film crew arranged at my house one weekend this April.

Think of Eastwood waiting for a cloudy day, the sky uniformly light gray, to shoot the scene with Thao gardening in Walt's back yard, each "coaching" the other ("You should quit. It's bad for you. I saw you cough up blood." "What do you want to do with your life, kid?" "Thinkin' about going to school, maybe?" "You ought date this YumYum, too."). Drudge work may be part of Thao's penance for his attempted theft, but the setting (diffuse light; lush basil leaves) affects our interpretation of the developing relationship that will save both Walt and his young pupil.

Once Walt leaves his yard and enters another cultural space he is shocked into self-knowledge. He makes some social blunders, submits to spiritual reading by the Hmong shaman (an appeal for him to confess his past mistakes and an accurate analysis of severe depression—the loss of taste and joy). Shaken, Walt confronts himself in the bathroom mirror in an echo of the earlier mirror scene before the robbery: "I have more in common with these Gooks than I do with my own miserable family." The temperature of each mini-scene shifts somewhat, but not as noticeably as when Walt descends stairs and enters the kitchen, where the moms and grandmas pile his plate with food.

Soft light shines through the two broad windows behind the table, enlarging the space and baptizing the area with a glow. Lights have been placed outside the windows to make the "sunlight" coming in more intense and yet diffuse and welcoming. The women have brought the unhappy stranger into their midst for a real birthday celebration. (Even better, the event itself—a ritual celebration—offsets the depression that often afflicts elderly immigrants in America! So it's a two-fer.)[4] Even more pertinent to *Gran Torino*'s redemptive movement, the meal follows Walt's recognition of what he holds in common with the Hmong, the "equality" that meals in the Early Church fostered: the "real identity" created among believers by the mystical partaking of the (symbolic) body and blood of Jesus the Christ. Shared being is reinforced by the shared meal.[5] (Bob Jewett's weekly Eucharist meals in Nebraska demonstrate the rich possibilities of meal and Scriptural study.)

Meal Scene/Major Turning Point

The second half of the movie launches the new romance between Thao and Youa (YumYum) and follows the blossoming friendship with Sue, Thao, and the young priest and the attempt to give Thao survival skills. Ethnic boundaries, Walt believes, can be crossed by "man talk." Further, Thao shows himself more than ready to adopt Walt's work ethic.

This is no sentimental movie with easy answers, though. Walt's violent revenge beating of one of the gang boys who burned Thao's face and stole his tools leads to escalated violence: the drive-by shooting of the Hmong family's house and Sue's brutal rape and beating. How will he and Thao respond? The anguished conversation between Thao and Walt and

---

4. *The New York Times* (August 31, 2009), A1. See also Ang Lee's *Pushing Hands* (1992).

5. Simmel, 134–5. Simmel goes several steps further by saying that the table ranks higher than the food itself. Food is material, but the gathering elevates all those who sit down together.

later Walt and the priest eerily echoes the tellings of the tale of the "Cut Whore" in *Unforgiven*. As Will Munny and his friend Ned debated their next move, the little priest asks, "What you gonna do, Mr. Kowalski?" We fear once more: violence begets more violence. The long debate takes place in almost total darkness; the priest acknowledges that in Walt's place, he, too, would get revenge.

The confessions toward which the film has been moving, take place after Walt has prepared for a ritual bloodbath (Travis Bickle in *Taxi Driver*, 1976) or a mass (the priest in *Diary of a Country Priest*, 1951).

Confession to Thao

Two more confessions, one pro forma, the other heartfelt.

Combination of darkness and light: Light from an unknown source etches Walt's figure when he arrives before the gang members' houses, defining the iconic gunfighter of old, standing on one leg like Eastwood the actor did in the Spaghetti Westerns as though a gun belt lay tautly across his hips in the practiced gunfighter's style. In the meantime, after a good hour spent with the new Walt as he builds his new family, Sue is abducted and raped. A distraught Walt ponders what to do; his new son, Thao, and even the mild parish priest, want bloody revenge.

Walt confesses, first to the priest, and then to his sidekick Thao, whom he has locked up in the basement. He sets out to confront the rapists.

When Walt appears, the lights in the windows of the buildings that surround the gang's house brighten and drumbeats begin to thunder under the images. Eastwood's cinematographer has lit the entire neighborhood to allow light to edge his body as he faces the gang and their guns. Witnesses (including the parish priest with whom Walt has battled throughout the movie and a policeman who is also Hmong) peer out to observe, record, and later testify.

Showdown Scene

In keeping with Eastwood's earlier films that emphasize witness (*High Plains Drifter*, *Unforgiven*), the innocent onlookers can no longer turn their faces away from the degraded condition of their neighborhood. They cannot save Walt, but they may be able to save others. The passivity of the nighttime crowd in *High Plains Drifter* has been re-imaged in *Gran Torino* not as vigilante justice but rather as the orderly investment of citizens, however diverse their background, in the stability of the rule of law and the health of their neighborhoods.[6]

Walt asks, "Gotta light?" as he holds up one of his coffin nails, a cigarette and replies to himself, "I've gotta light." Saying his Hail Marys, he pulls out the lighter he had preserved since his war days, etched with the insignia of his lost battalion. Instead of a Magnum .44, the most powerful gun on earth, Walt clasps the lighter that had lit the millions of cigarettes that consumed his lungs. But now, it lights his way toward new life.

Etched in light, bullets rip through his body as they must have torn the Preacher's flesh in *Pale Rider*. He falls in slow motion into a messianic death pose. As he bleeds to death on the lawn, the camera slowly pans out, revealing Walt framed as if he were Christ himself, arms outstretched with blood trailing down his wrists.

The light changes direction as we see Walt's body laid out prayerfully, recalling yet another body—a young Japanese soldier from *Flags of Our Fathers*, a bayonet sticking through his chest, etched in a harsher light than this but evoking similar sorrow at a life lost.

Death Scene

The film ends out-of-doors, not in any of the confined spaces we've seen in the film, but with Thao and Walt's old dog Daisy driving down the Grosse Point highway with smiles on their faces. The once-despised and weak immigrant, heir of the "real" America of openness and generosity, heir of Walt's love, drives a mythic symbol of Americana, the Gran Torino.

ANTIPHONY AND ECHOES

Bookends: Funeral of Walt's Wife/Walt's funeral

- Young priest as naïve twit/priest with a beer and new understanding of violence;

---

6. Thanks to the members of my Northwestern University class on Eastwood in Winter of 2009, who provided perceptive insights into Eastwood's accomplishments in this movie: the metaphorical significance of the white truck; the creation of inclusion and community—"from lone man to family man"; Walt's ritual preparations for death; the parallel confessions; the complementary elements in *Unforgiven* and *Gran Torino*, with each film exploring the outer edges of human nature.

- The funeral meal at Walt's house/the baptismal meal at the house of the new neighbors next door, an extended Hmong family;
- Walt's sons, figures out of *commedia dell'Arte*, their faces lit like zanni figures (fool)/the authentic relationships Walt develops with his young neighbors next door, Thao and Sue;
- Walt's hidden trunk with his war medal, basement; kids' parochialism/Walt's hidden secret;
- After Hmong meal, basement and new romance;
- Walt's granddaughter with her dead cell phone/Walt's new neighbor, Sue, with her "grounded sense of self;"
- Walt's rifle/Walt's lighter;
- Walt the lonely man, fully armed/Walt the family man, unarmed;
- Walt looking over his fence at his new neighbors and growling about their primitive customs/Walt and Thao working in the garden/Walt barbeque in his own back yard with Sue, Thao, Youa; and
- Confessions: layered and echoed—the false ones to the priest/the true one to Thao.

Sara Anson Vaux
Presented at Garrett-Evangelical Theological Seminary
April 30, 2010

9

How Do I Know Thee?

Jan van Eys, MD

WE HUMANS ARE OF one piece—substance and spirit, body and soul. The components of our being are separate but inseparable. Our mind, our spirit, our soul, can only communicate and interact through our body, using our body's capabilities. That is our human limitation; that is how we were created.

Our bodies are wondrously and gloriously made. Through our bodies we have capabilities to remain aware of the world around us. We call these capabilities our senses. Through our senses we are aware of what is in our environment, how much is there, is there more or less than before, where is it, is it changing in time or in place.[1] These are data our body needs to survive in, move through, and interact with the world around us.

KNOWING THROUGH SENSES

Traditionally we talk about five senses: hearing, vision, smell, touch, and proprioception. Some have subsets, some are richer than others, some are essential for survival and others are not.

- Proprioception tells us where our body is in space—it makes our motion coordinated. It includes balance, a function partially carried by our ears in the vestibular system. Total loss makes our body unmanageable but the loss does not kill it.

---

1. This summary of sense tasks is taken from: Neurosciences for Kids; http://faculty.washington.edu/chudler/chsense.html.

- Touch includes pain and temperature discernment. It makes us aware, of our environment by testing. It allows us to learn to distinguish between dangerous and safe contacts. It makes our skin the largest sensory organ in our body. Children born without sense of pain often kill themselves unwittingly, because they never learn from past experience what is dangerous and what is not.[2]

- Smell helps us to discern individuality between elements in our environment. There is a separate sense of taste. However, that is limited to only three types of perceptions: bitter versus sweet; salty versus sour; and the ability to discern glutamic acid and glutamine salts (such as MSG). We call that sense umami. However, the vast preponderance of the sensation of tasting of food relies on our sense of smell. If you lose your sense of smell food will taste bland and uninteresting. Smell also plays an important role in sexual attraction and gender discernment. It is a vastly underrated sense, but the loss of smell is not lethal, nor even a major handicap to an individual.

- Sight is the sense we most appreciate. We rely on sight to describe our environment. Through it we grade our environment esthetically. We can judge where objects are in space and where in the environment we find ourselves. It helps us to distinguish objects and people that feel and sound similar. Many animals use smell for that, but we have not honed that skill. We even order our society largely through reliance on sight. It has become important for communication between humans. But sight is not essential for survival, especially in a larger community of humans.

- Hearing is like sight. It allows things and people to be located without being seen. It allows direct communication between persons. Loss is also not a major threat to survival.

Thus it may seem that only touch/pain and proprioception are the essential senses for survival. Yet survival so far was used only to mean continued bodily existence. But we are body and soul. Our consciousness needs more to thrive than mere survival.

---

2. The disease is Familial Dysautonomia. It is also known as Riley-Day Syndrome. In those children the symptoms get worse over time. More than 60 percent die in their first 20 years.

Our body grows and matures over time. It learns to resist, to avoid noxious stimuli and to pursue pleasant sensations. It acquires the ability and desire to procreate. Even though that learning uses our senses, all that can happen without full consciousness. The mind can be only minimally engaged in the pursuit of comfort and safety.

But eyes do more than see and ears do more than hear. Once it dawns on us that self is more than mere existence, our world broadens and our needs grow. We begin to imagine that the other bodies out there that we smell, see, and hear, also include a self, albeit a strange other. We can learn details about the physical body of the other, but the inner self is hidden. We begin to imagine who that other self is. First we imagine that it is just like our own self. Our only standard of normalcy is ourselves.[3] But as we gather clues from our senses, we are forced to conclude that selves are more varied.

We see the other body. That body communicates to us largely through smell. But when the mind communicates it does so largely by sound and, to a lesser degree, by sight. In order for sound to be meaningful humans created language.

KNOWING THROUGH LANGUAGE

Language is a construct of the mind. It is not inherent in the body like smell and appearance are. Our bodily adornments often are used as signals, but they are weak ones. While we can deduce to some degree the type of mind the other self has by the other's actions, we can only create a real picture of the other's minds by how they describe the world they see. It is true that the language can be conveyed visually by signs or the written word. In fact AMESLAN (American Sign Language) is a distinct language in its own right and can be used as a substitute for oral communication. But the primary and default method of communication between selves is oral. In fact, that is the way we develop, teach, and learn a common language.

Teaching a language could be done otherwise. However, the story of Helen Keller, the child who became deaf and blind after a short but serious illness at age 18 months, tells us it is extremely difficult. Helen Keller's tutor, Anne Sullivan, managed to instill language by capitalizing on the fine discrimination possible in the sense of touch. Mrs. Sullivan

---

3. See: Jan van Eys, "Who Then is Normal," *Church and Society* 78 (1, 1982), 8–19.

was aptly called the miracle worker.⁴ Helen Keller's story richly illustrates the necessity of language to discover the other self in a stranger.

We need each other to thrive. We need to respect the other in order to be able to respect ourselves. We need to imagine the mind of the stranger to be able to construct an understanding of our own mind. We need that to become reasonable and rational human beings, who can imagine and convey a concept of a creator. We need to have a reasonably clear image of the other in order to trust the other. If we don't, we are just bodies surviving on instinct and suspicion of the world in which we find ourselves. All that requires language.

It follows then that hearing is the sense that is most important to be and to remain human. To become blind isolates one somewhat from the physical world but to become deaf threatens to isolate one from the community of human souls. That sense of loneliness creates despair.

Human minds can conceive and deduce the existence of God. While we depict our imagery in art, we also sing about it. Music requires hearing and music is a very early art form.

The importance of the senses and the supremacy of hearing is marvelously summarized by George Bernard Shaw in his play, Saint Joan.⁵ When Joan of Arc is tried for heresy, she is coerced and seduced into a confession, in order to save her life. When she finds out that condemns her to life imprisonment, she snatches her signed confession from the judges and tears it up. She then gives this marvelous and passionate speech:

> My voices were right! Yes, they told me you were fools and that I was not to listen to your fine words nor trust your charity. You think that life is nothing but not being stone dead. It is not the bread and water that I fear. I can live on bread; when have I asked for more? It is no hardship to drink water, if the water be clean. Bread has no sorrow for me and water no affliction. But to shut me from the light of the sky and the sight of the field and flowers, to chain my feet so that I can never ride again with the soldiers nor climb the hills, to make me breathe foul damp darkness, and keep

---

4. The appellation of "The Miracle Worker," given to Anne Sullivan, was coined by Mark Twain, who was a great admirer of Helen Keller. The play, TV movies, and films were based on Helen Keller's autobiography (written with Anne Sullivan and John A. Macy), *The Story of My Life;* New York: Doubleday, Page, and Company, 1903).

5. George Bernard Shaw, Saint Joan. Scene VI. The play was written in 1924. I used the online text found in Project Gutenberg, Australia, a site where free e-books can be found and can be downloaded.

> from me everything that brings me back to the love of God when your wickedness and foolishness tempts me to hate Him, all this is worse than the furnace in the Bible that was heated seven times. I could do without my warhorse, I could drag about in a skirt, I could let the banner and the trumpets and the knights and soldiers pass me and leave me behind as they leave the other women, if only I could still hear the wind in the trees, the larks in the sunshine, the young lambs crying through the healthy frost, and the blessed, blessed church bells that send my angel voices floating to me on the wind. But without these things I cannot live and by you wanting to take them away from me or from any human creature, I know that your counsel is of the devil and that mine is of God.

We may not hear the voices Joan of Arc did, but the human voice coming lovingly from another person can tell us what God is like. Once we know Him, our sight sees God's handiwork, our touch changes from discerning an obstacle into a gesture of love. Having no hearing, we would start as Helen Keller, a near uncontrollable animal-like child. If we lose hearing later in life we miss the contact with the minds of the others who have shaped our world with us. We ought to listen to Francis Poulenc's chamber opera, La Voix Humaine (the human voice) to understand the despair of losing the words of someone who is very necessary to your existence.[6]

Losing hearing does not cause bodily death, but it does deprive our soul from growing together with our human spirit peers. We frequently do things and go places videre viderique—to see and be seen. But that is self-indulgence at best and self aggrandizement at worst. Above all we desperately want to hear and be heard, lest we find ourselves alone and frustrated. Losing hearing is one of the greatest losses we can suffer.

Jan van Eys
April 2010

---

6. Francis Poulenc, *La Voix Humaine*. Written in 1930. It is a monologue over a telephone by a woman trying to reconnect with her lover.

10

Giving Sight to the Blind

Kimberly Curnyn, MD

INTERFAITH AND INTERDISCIPLINARY JOURNEY

LET ME START WITH religion. My background is varied. I grew up in a Roman Catholic Church, went to mass every Sunday. The only thing I really remember about scripture or the Bible, because we really didn't read the Bible at home, is that we had on it the coffee table and every generation signed it. But Catholics didn't read the Bible. So we waited until Sunday morning and we heard Old and New Testament gospel, and I do distinctively remember the stories of the blind being able to see. The miracle stories in the Bible, no matter how old you are, catch you by the heart and make you think either, in a philosophical sense, "I want to see, I want to experience that," or if you are suffering an infirmity or habitual illness or a family member is ill, you may want to have the sense of a miraculous cure you want to be part of or you want to participate in. Doctors with patients are always in the realm the Bible calls healing.

So, I grew up and went on to Notre Dame. Forty years ago, there wasn't a lot of interfaith dialogue, especially at Notre Dame, until the year I showed up. I was in one of the first entry classes open to women, so the campus was already in a dither about everything. Then Richard McBrien wrote two series, two volumes of Catholicism, volumes one and two. Neither ever passed the papal approval. I don't know if you remember who was a part of the approval back then, but in the "congregation of the faith," but he is now the pope. It created quite a stir. He came in and he was considered pretty heretical in shaking up student's minds.

The next person I worked with was John Dunne. He came out of the Catholic tradition, but fell in love with the Hindu Sophia tradition and started exploring this development that Catholics had had with mystical experience. And he would talk to his students, "here we are in the valley and our God is on the mountain and God wants to be in the valley with us every bit as much as we want to be on the mountain with Him." He would use biblical stories of how we are trying to interact in each others' lives and how we are trying to have this common bond of not only spiritual and mental connection, but a physical connection. Our conference has touched on this sort of craving to be a part of the light.

The last person I worked with was even more controversial. It was Stanley Hauerwas. I remember a spring day like this at Notre Dame, the windows were open, and I was sitting in a seat at the back, and he would always call me the "Catholic," because I was sitting in the back seat. He said, "I bet when you go to church you sit in the last pew every week." But anyway, he pulled out the Bible, and we are not as used to that as Catholics, and he opened the book, and he read:

> Two blind men followed (him), crying out, "Son of David, have pity on us!" When he entered the house, the blind men approached him and Jesus said to them, "Do you believe that I can do this?" "Yes, Lord," they said to him. Then he touched their eyes and said, "Let it be done for you according to your faith." And their eyes were opened. (Matt 9:27–30a)

Then Stanley Hauerwas—while closing the Bible and slamming it on the desk—said, "Damn, those guys could see again." I remember thinking, this is not just a nice story that I am going to remember from Sunday gospels, but the idea is that Hauerwas was so convinced that we're living this narrative, this theology is experiential, that years later, generations later, we have got to carry on the story and remember that there is a physical element to God's transcendence and presence among us.

I left Notre Dame and ended up at the University of Illinois. There were two main people at the University of Illinois. Of course, Dr. Ken Vaux. I sought refuge with him in the surgical department, because when I went to the philosophy side on campus, the chairman there said, "Well, all I can say is that if you believe in a monotheistic God, then we have nothing else to talk about." And, I thought I was interfaith-trained. I had worked with Protestant, Methodist, Mennonites, like Dr. John Yoder, and yet here I was not quite fulfilling what they expected as a philosopher. When working with Dr. Vaux, I was so impressed by the fact that he was not intimidated by the clinical language. I know that many of us in medicine are thrown off by the philosophical and theological language that we forget sometimes that our colleagues, the ones in the humanities are intimated by our language. And every day I ran rounds, he was there learning about dopamine drips, end of life, brain death criteria—and he actually had an honest dialogue with the faculty, residents, and students at that time. It was inspiring, and I think that kind of ability to dialogue with several biomedical arenas is what led him to do his spiritual work to organize this kind of conference. The other interesting thing was he was looking at allocation of resources much earlier than the rest of us. It was a new age. We are talking about dilemmas, new machines, and new techniques and he would be asking, "What is happening in the rest of the world. How are we using our resources here, especially the well-trained U.S. physicians? Are we looking at a broader scale?"

Another thing Dr. Vaux brought in to conversation was individual history. He respected the patient. And you have to understand until the late 60's early 70's, when a very important idea emerged about the "patient as a person," physicians really didn't talk to the patient as a person. They saw the patient as a disease state, and they their international acumen made the correct diagnosis and offered the correct cure. But, not everybody got better when the right diagnosis was made and the right cure was given. And I think the year when Dr. Vaux was working with the residents we were starting to see that, people were tapping into something else. Whether it was their personal Hindu faith, or they were allowed to pray the way they wanted to, or somebody avoided certain food types—if you allowed that person to tap into that history and respect that in the matter of the setting, those patients often did far better. It was amazing, because he tapped into that and again much earlier than most people did. A lot was written about the religious or faith tradition —the value of heritage of persons being important—in the 80's and he was doing that in the early 80's or late 70's.

Also, Dr. Vaux brought to the conversation the concern for wellness. The idea he brought to his medical students is that he didn't want to see you exhausted and confused in the hour, he want to know you, as a doctor, were living a life of wellness. And that meant understanding your own spiritual background, what you needed to do in this world; he fostered a healthy group of physicians in his training program.

My other wonderful role model is my father, Dr. Arnold Curnyn, who is here at the conference. I was coming out of this academic setting and doing a PhD in philosophy. Should I go into the religious life? I was all over the place. My dad, who was practicing ophthalmologist in the Northwest suburbs of Chicago, a very humble man, just took care of patients. And then occasionally he would go overseas and take care of patients. Part of me was thinking, "Well, you know, how much good can you do in the world just seeing patients?" Well, one of the trips we took was to Africa, and at that point I was looking into sociology, social medicine. And I saw my dad leaving the operating room and his patients walking out—this was in Africa where, to be a candidate for surgery, you had to be totally blind. You also had to have ultra-light perception because there was a scarcity of resources. His patients were walking out literally like people in the Bible—being able to see. They were amazed, they had not seen in years before their surgery. And they could see. I remember getting back to Chicago and calling Ken and saying, "I think I made up my mind what I am going to do." Because ophthalmology is the closest you can get, in my mind in medicine, to merge the spiritual seeking, the spiritual enlightenment that we all want. Here we find ability to share that with another human being.

SIGHT AND BLINDNESS IN MEDICINE

So I look back with gratitude, so when Ken gave me this topic, "Giving Sight to the Blind" I couldn't say no. There are so many different directions I could go. So, I first looked to see what is in my old ophthalmology literature. Let me try looking at these issues, historically. What did medicine have to say about blindness and spirituality? What did the biblical traditions say? There was Archives of Ophthalmology, one of our leading journals, and in 1933, Benjamin Gordon wrote an article, "Ophthalmology in the Bible and in the Talmud."[1] I thought that it was interesting for a physician to try to look at the historical data, where ophthalmology as a blindness-preventing or sight-saving specialty, was located historically. A

---

1. Benjamin Gordon, "Ophthalmology in the Bible and in the Talmud," *Archives of Ophthalmology* 1933; 9(5): 751–788.

couple of years later, the *British Journal of Ophthalmology* had an article, "Blindness, Eye Diseases, and Their Causes in the Land of Canaan."[2] If you think about it, in the 30's, X-rays were just coming into wide use and they were starting to X-ray mummies. One of the things that they noticed was that mummies, even if they had a deformed eye, it wasn't removed. Here in the U.S., if people have trauma to eye or the eye has a very serious retinal detachment and the eye is "blind," you tend to remove it for cosmetic appearance and put in an artificial eye. These mummies had these retained eyes and many of them were suffering from some form of blindness. A lot of the mummies actually had larvae from river blindness from flies that cause the disease. One of Dr. Vaux's articles in the early 80's talked of a drug, probably costing 2 or 10 cents a dose, which could be distributed along the rivers to prevent river blindness. For ten thousand dollars, you could save five or six entire cities along the river per year from any kind of blindness. If we look back at the Egyptian age to this article, "Disease and Their Causes in the Land of Canaan," the infection was there. People were going blind from the infection.

Another study came out more recently in the Survey of Ophthalmology. There was an article, "Was Saint Paul Struck Blind and Converted by Lightning?"[3] It was an ophthalmologist who wrote it and who gave a physical description of the impact lightning can have on our system. What will the electrical damage do to the visual system, thought processes, and the time frame for recovery? Now the conclusion of it, what if we did find out that Saint Paul was hit by lightning and this was some type of physical response to the environment? Paul has a huge place in our history, but what this physician was hoping to say was he could actually legitimate the biblical story of the conversion of Saint Paul by a physical explanation. And I was thinking this morning of migraines; if a mystic have migraines that may color their experience, does that mean the experience is less real? Perhaps such persons have physical phenomena that enhance or open the door into another experience. That is what this ophthalmologist was hoping for when he published this article back in 1994.

---

2. "Blindness, Eye Disease and Their Causes in the Land of Canaan," *British Journal of Ophthalmology* 1935; 19; 548–576.

3. "Was Saint Paul Struck Blind by Lightning?" *Survey of Ophthalmology* Volume 39, Issue 2, September-October 1994, 151–160.

The most recent connection between light and the role of ophthalmology and questioning spiritual light is in Archives of Ophthalmology. They ask, "Is the perception of light useful to the blind patient?"[4] When children are born blind or they have tumors in their eye or if they have severe trauma to the eye and the eye is ugly and dark, surgeons tend to remove the eye because they think it is better for the person. Yet, we look historically and other civilizations have left the eyes in. This author talked to people, even if the eye was blind—meaning they really had no usable vision to move around—they might have just an inkling of light. These patients felt they were better off with a deformed eye with just a hint of light than without the eye. It is a very dramatic article. He goes to a blind school where children are born blind or become blind all the time. He interviewed patients. They definitely felt that they were considered blind by the world's standards, but they felt they had some light, some perception. Now there is a quote from the last article, "So if your eye is sound, your body will be full of light; but if your eye is not sound, your whole body will be full of darkness" (Matt 6:22–23). It is a sort of struggle, this light and darkness. And the question is if we do have sight, are we better, are we spiritually more alive? There are so many levels to think about. The blind are also very concerned to be affirmed as persons.

HUMAN VISION SYSTEM

Today, I just want to consider the anatomical and physical portion of vision. In the study of human vision system and the recovery of sight, whether we use nutritional aspects, medical aspects, or surgical care—concern the profession of ophthalmology.

We are so use to thinking that the visual system is just the eyeball. That's the organ we think of when we get measured for glasses or when the eye exam is done. They eye is actually the extension of our central nervous system (CNS). Even more importantly, our CNS actually has binocular vision. So, when you think about it, yes you can have monocular vision—one eye does well—but the vision system was designed so that we're meant to have binocular vision. We tend to get this physical sense of three-dimensional view of the world. Any type of loss of vision of physical light is considered blindness. Now, when we look at the anatomy,

---

4. "Is Perception of Light Useful to the Blind Patient?" *Archives of Ophthalmology* 1998:116, 236–238.

we know there is the eye, and most of us learned about the eye in biology in high school. The eye is what we as ophthalmologists feel comfortable that we can restore sight in the cornea, the outer layer of the eye. We now can do physical transplants on from the cadaver to the individual. Replacing the lens inside the eye, which develops cataracts, is now a very straightforward procedure, we are removing the cloudy lens and putting in a clear lens. Where we get into trouble is this neurological connection from the optic nerve back to the brain.

So again, when we take a look at the cornea, the lens, and the retina, it is accessible to the surgeon and it is on the surface and we have wonderful medical therapies and surgical therapies to cure blindness in humans. Once we get deeper into the retina, perhaps you have friends who have suffered from macular degeneration or retina detachments. These are very difficult diseases to handle because the retina is so extremely complicated. We have rods and cones in the retina. The rods give us peripheral vision and the cones give us our central vision. And the cones, when you think about it, actually conduct different layers of light rays. So we get a process of light in the cones in our retina in our macula. It goes blue, green, and red, depending on the light rays. Once this information is conducted from the retina, it is then constructed or tracked back to the brain. There is one other missing piece that we are finally starting to appreciate called opsins. Opsins absorb a light particle. Now, this is fascinating because it makes you sort of re-vibrate with the spiritual discussion we had this morning. And it will send a signal. And we are wondering now if there is another form of vision that our body's interprets. Is there an additional element of light perception other than the one typical visual form plays?

Once we get from the retina to the optic nerve, things get more complicated. There are axons that go to different areas of the lateral geniculate that helps process vision. We also find that some of the pathways from our eyes control what the sense of motion is, our position in the world, and our interaction with the world. Then there is a last group, this melanopsin that has ganglion cells that travel to the pretectum and sends this unconscious vision. Someone who is blind, if they had such great damage to their eye or they had the eye removed, would lose the ability to have natural circular lifecycles. They find they have disrupted sleep cycles when they go blind. There is another sensory perception of light in our body we are just starting to uncover.

Again the pathways go back to the back of the brain, and ultimately end at the visual cortex. The visual cortex is where our information of vision is stored, where our sense of shapes and movement are stored in the back of our brain. Ophthalmologists work at this fascinating portion of the visual system, but really vision involves the whole neurological system.

BLINDNESS AND SIGHT RECOVERY

There are four kinds of cases of blindness that constantly stump me and amaze me. And when I talk to my residents, they sometimes say, "Oh, Dr. Curnyn, you're doing that philosophy kind of stuff again." They know how to remove a cataract, fix glaucoma, and repair retinal detachment. But I ask them other questions. First, when you see a baby born with cataracts, if these cataracts are completely mature and they are totally blinding the light input into the child's brain, if you do not remove that cataract before the child is four months old, that child is irreversibly blind for the rest of their life. They never form those appropriate pathways. They never form those optical tracks. When I travel internationally, I work with a group I call ORBIS. A group of nurses who goes ahead of me to India, Vietnam, or wherever we will be going, and they screen the children. We know that 30 percent of blind children in developed countries have that condition because of congenital cataracts. As they screen them, they will find 20 kids with congenital cataracts and that those who are over a certain age have already developed this wondering eye nystagmus—meaning their visual system is trying to find light. Then we know the game is over. Even if we take those cataracts out at that point, these children will never see again. And it becomes a waste of resources. So we have to remove the cataracts of the children who are young enough that if we get light into their eye, their visual system will develop, and they can avoid river blindness. It is a sad thing to have to turn some of these parents away with children, but we know that cataracts are that detrimental to the development of the visual system of a child. In an adult, who has had normal vision their whole life, cataracts encroach on their vision and limit things. We remove the cataract and get back to where they were when they were younger. That doesn't happen to children. The searching eye nystagmus, is fascinating. The parents who have children born impaired, a lot of times will pick it up before the pediatrician. Because they will say, "It is just so odd, all they do is look at the one light or the one window." They think it is a behavioral thing where we know the visual system is trying to mature. Now, when we screen these babies, what we are looking for is the white in the center of the pupil. When it is completely white, it adds to the capacity, so the light rays aren't getting into the eye. And again, it is devastating to the family when you tell them it is too late to operate on the child's eyes.

The next disease, is mind boggling to me, is called congenital leber's neurosis. Leber's is actually the diagnosis given to Derek Lee's (a major league baseball player) daughter a few years ago. Perhaps you are a diehard fan. Derek started a movement because this is a devastating disease. When these kids are born, they look completely normal. Their eyes are normal, they have normal reflexes on their cornea, but they start an interesting behavior at a young age. They gouge and rub their eyes. These children are born with pigment missing in their retina, so they never develop any of the connections between the retina and the brain. They are totally blind. They have no light perception. They stimulate, or try to stimulate light. If you have tried to rub your eyes too hard and you see these sparkles of light and you dent your eye, but these kids will do it all day long. They will sit there for hours like this. A lot of times this is why their parents will bring them to the doctor saying, "I don't know what to do. They won't keep their hands away from their eyes." Now we're hoping—with the help of Derek Lee who started a foundation—that we can find a genetic recovery that we can use genes to turn on the retina and the retina pigment, in turn. The trouble is, if you let them keep rubbing their eyes, they will actually damage their physical eyeball itself and their cornea will become warped. They will get a disease called caracomas. The other things is these kids will rub so hard, that the orbal fat that supports our eyeballs in the skull, atrophies and the eyeballs sink back and will get in a abnormal position. You might have seen that blind adults, have a very sunken eyeball appearance. So, even though these kids look normal and functionally are blind, unless we find a genetic cure, we won't be able to reverse it. Surprisingly, our cure may come from dogs. There is actually a cell line of dogs that have the same leber's diseases. And, if a child matches it what we are hoping, because studies are taking place right now, perhaps we can turn on the retina and restore their vision.

The third disease is one that frustrates me with no end. It's a macular disease, and the most common form we think of in this country is macular degeneration. What happens is this center portion of the retina, the cones, basically degenerates. You lose your central vision. You see a little blur and then suddenly your vision is gone. For anyone who wants to drive, losing your central vision takes away your ability to transcript signs. People who love to read lose their reading ability. It can be so extreme, an entire area is lost, and people just move around with their far peripheral vision. Luckily, there are two stages of this degeneration. One is the slowly progressive type for which the only hope we have is probably nutritional support. When I went back to school no one taught vitamins or nutrition because they thought that was sort of voodoo. But, we found that a healthy diet of vitamins A, B, E, and zinc can slow down the degeneration of the retina size. They also found that sometimes the retina is trying so hard to heal itself when it is degenerating, that it is actually growing new blood vessels into the retina. It is almost like a physiological adaptation that the body is trying to heal itself, but the new blood vessels break open and bleed, and this is what we call wet degeneration. We have been able to discover that one of the key chemotherapy drugs we use for colon cancer can actually be used for wet degeneration.

The trouble is that pharmaceutical companies—who charge $25 for a large vial of chemotherapy agent called methotrexate used for cancer therapy—did not want ophthalmologists to inject it into the eye to save vision. Since you probably can do 200 injections out of the big vial—they don't make much money from that—the pharmaceutical companies said "no." They decided to re-label that drug as an eye drug and charge $1,200 a vial. And so goes our own healthcare system, and it drives me crazy because we have the people who can afford the labeled, FDA-approved, monocular degeneration chemotherapy drug, and there are those who can't. And if you have a doctor, who trained at the University of Illinois under Ken Vaux, those are the doctors who will say, "I'll still get you the other stuff." It works efficiently, but they have to do it basically on the sly because the pharmacies are instructed not to sell the cheaper version, or the larger vile drug, to ophthalmologists. Now, if you pay attention to a large set of monocular degeneration cases, you can see how you're missing the center, 90 percent of your vision. Again, the brain wants to see. There is this innate tendency of the human body, created by the idea of Dr. Won, I really believe it. What will happen to these patients, and it happens to as many as 33 percent of these with severe degeneration, is they get a Charles Romain phenomenon. Where the brain will pull out images, stored in the occipital cortex and plug it into this box that is missing.

This happens because the brain wants to get the big picture and it knows it is missing something. So, I remember when I was in my first week of practice and a little old lady came in with bad degeneration and said, "I don't know how to say this, but I am seeing angels." Again, coming off my philosophy, theology background, I think, "You're seeing angels. This is wonderful. What are you seeing?" She was experiencing this Charles Romain phenomenon. And about three weeks later, I had someone come in and say she was seeing ducks and umbrellas. These images can be crazy. Some people see double, some people see food, some people see anything, but it is this cortex response in the brain trying to fill in the missing pieces. If doctors aren't savvy to it, the patients are very frightened. They think they are going crazy. They are having true visual hallucinations, but it is a response to a true physiological problem. Again, you start to think, how marvelous is the human organism as it tries to heal—to see light.

The last category of blindness I want to bring up is called Anton's syndrome. When persons have a normal eye, normal optic nerve, normal brain, but in the very back of the brain in the occipital lobe, they have a stroke or some kind of disease or some trauma—this occurs. These people will go totally blind and they are very calm about it. They will get up in the morning and go to the bathroom and bump the wall, and their husband will say, "Honey, what are you doing?" They say, "I am going to the bathroom." And the husband says, "You're hitting the wall." She says, "Oh, yeah." And not in the sense that, "Oh my God, I am blind. I can't find the door to the bathroom." These people are calm. They come to the doctor's office and we test them and sure enough they don't have any light perception. When we do an MRI or CT scan of the head, we find out that they have either had a total stroke in the back of their brain—sufficient to lose vision—or they have a kind of an ischemic event where the blood vessels are swollen. Many times you can't reverse it. It's amazing to me that they remain very calm people. They go through life, people lead them where they wish to go, they visit, they listen to music and they never get angry or upset about being blind. It is an amazing hope of mine that there is a gift of God involved in these compensations.

BIBLICAL NARRATIVES OF BLINDNESS AND SIGHT

What I want to do in conclusion is to look at some of the biblical stories. Again, I'm not saying that I found a physical reason for the biblical stories, but I think I've found something for us to think about. God is coming down from the mountain and we are trying to get to HHhim. There is a connection on God's incarnation in this world. Now as we began this conference of light and sight, we had this discussion this morning that God created light (Gen 1:4), God created man in His image (Gen 1:27), man and female, He created them. Now if we look at the Gospel of Healing the Blind. The first case I want to bring up is healing the blind man since birth (John 9:1–12). It was in John. The man has been named "Celidonius." I don't know if there are any Eastern Orthodox believers here, but I guess in the sixth week of Easter, they will celebrate the man who is saved from blindness. The stories always say he is blind from birth. Therefore, think back to the case of children who have congenital cataracts, where they have no visual system that has developed and allows them to see. And a lot of times, they don't know what they are missing. And in the story of the healing of the man going blind it reads,

> As he passed by he saw a man blind from birth. His disciples asked him, "Rabbi, who sinned, this man or his parents, that he was born blind?" Jesus answered, "Neither he nor his parents sinned; it is so that the works of God might be made visible through him. We have to do the works of the one who sent me while it is day. Night is coming when no one can work. While I am in the world, I am the light of the world." When he had said this, he spat on the ground and made clay with the saliva, and smeared the clay on his eyes, and said to him, "Go wash in the Pool of Siloam" (which means "sent"). So he went and washed, and came back able to see. (John 9:1–7)

The one way Jesus cured the blind man is awesome. I thought about this earlier. We think about our origin as a creation of God either from red clay, the earth, or the mud, from water. I never put this together until this morning. But isn't it interesting that Jesus went through the actual physical motion to wet the earth and the mud and use that to cure a person who is blind since birth? We know now that being blind since birth means you haven't developed any visual cortex and yet this person was able to see. So, it is amazing. All we can say is that wonderful narratives illustrate that wonder.

How about the two men near the gate of Jericho?[5]

---

5. Matthew 20:29–34 is similar to the narrative shown here. One of the differences is that in Matthew, there are two blind men instead of one.

> Now as he approached Jericho a blind man was sitting by the roadside begging, and hearing a crowd going by, he inquired what was happening. They told him, "Jesus of Nazareth is passing by." He shouted, "Jesus, Son of David,8 have pity on me!" The people walking in front rebuked him, telling him to be silent, but he kept calling out all the more, "Son of David, have pity on me!" Then Jesus stopped and ordered that he be brought to him; and when he came near, Jesus asked him, "What do you want me to do for you?" He replied, "Lord, please let me see." Jesus told him, "Have sight; your faith has saved you." He immediately received his sight and followed him, giving glory to God. When they saw this, all the people gave praise to God. (Luke 18:35–43)

They wanted to get their vision back whereas the man born blind, the crowd brought him to him. They wanted to use him as an example. To say, "Hey Jesus, what did he do wrong? What did his parents do wrong?" The guys at the gate sought out Jesus, they had heard he was doing miracles. They wanted their vision back. So, you have to expect they had something like a degenerative disease, like a macular degeneration. They had experienced vision and wanted it back. And this is where Jesus did not use water, did not use clay, he just asked for faith. He said, "'Have sight; your faith has saved you.' He immediately received his sight and followed him, giving glory to God." (Luke 18:42–43a) Remember the wonderful picture by El Greco talking about the man going blind. And you can see everybody watching and Jesus is actually physically healing and curing the blindness.

Now the last two I want to finish up with are single stories of individual men that are both in Mark. The first one, Christ took the man out of town and actually spit and put his hands on his eyes (Mark 8:22–25). He used a physical element again, contacting the person. And it is interesting, it didn't work. When you think about it, it is sort of how you feel sometimes when you have lasex or cataract surgery when the patient comes back and is like, "Oh it is better Doc, but I thought I would see a little better than this. So, Jesus put his hands on him and the man said, "I see men as trees." So the vision was coming back, but it wasn't quite right, so God put his hands, Christ put his hands on again, and then he could see crystal clear. So, again, I love these variations of physical healing, this physical recovery of blindness.

And the last individual was Bartimaeus, which translates to Son of Timeaus (Mark 10:46–52). Again, we are talking about platonic tradition earlier this morning. And when you think about it, Timeaus is the one who delivered the message that sight is the foundation of knowledge. This is the only man who is really named in the Bible of somebody who was healed. The other individuals were given a name later. When we take a look at Mark 10, he was an amazing man. "Bartimaeus, a blind man, the son of Timaeus, sat by the roadside begging. On hearing that it was Jesus of Nazareth, he began to cry out and say, 'Jesus, son of David, have pity on me.' And many rebuked him, telling him to be silent. But he kept calling out all the more, 'Son of David, have pity on me.' Jesus stopped and said, 'Call him.' So they called the blind man, saying to him, 'Take courage; get up, he is calling you'" (Mark 10:46b–49). Of course here is an individual, he wanted to be healed, he wanted to be seen, and he had that opportunity and so many of us are like, "Uh, maybe I don't want to ask for it now." "He threw aside his cloak, sprang up, and came to Jesus. Jesus said to him in reply, 'What do you want me to do for you?' The blind man replied to him, 'Master, I want to see.' Jesus told him, 'Go your way; your faith has saved you.' immediately he received his sight and followed him on the way" (Mark 10:50–52). And I think that is the most wonderful story. We have the chance to see, if we want to. We know our sources we can turn to.

Now the last story, this goes back to 2 Kings. And remember when I told you about the Anton's syndrome where the occipital lobe is damaged and people are calm about being blind. When I read this story in 2 Kings, this one amazes me. I don't know if you remember this story at all where Elisha prayed for the soldiers to be blinded. They are amidst a war and the soldiers are trying to track him down. And Elisha said,

> "Our side outnumbers theirs." Then he prayed, "O LORD, open his eyes, that he may see." And the LORD opened the eyes of the servant, so that he saw the mountainside filled with horses and fiery chariots around Elisha. When the Arameans came down to get him, Elisha prayed to the LORD, "Strike this people blind, I pray you." And in answer to the prophet's prayer the LORD struck them blind. Then Elisha said to them: "This is the wrong road, and this is the wrong city. Follow me! I will take you to the man you want." And he led them to Samaria. When they entered Samaria, Elisha prayed, "O LORD, open their eyes that they may see."
> (2 Kings 6:16b–20a)

Now imagine, the talent of armies, big, scrappy, strong men, suddenly being blind and say, "Oh, we're on the wrong road." Anton's syndrome said they would. Was there an ischemic event, something going on that affected these people similarly at the same time? So they herd the soldiers into the city. And I love that they did get their sight back.

> The LORD opened their eyes, and they saw that they were inside Samaria. When the king of Israel saw them, he asked, "Shall I kill them, my father?" "You must not kill them," replied Elisha. "Do you slay those whom you have taken captive with your sword or bow? Serve them bread and water. Let them eat and drink, and then go back to their master." The king spread a great feast for them. When they had eaten and drunk he sent them away, and they went back to their master. No more Aramean raiders came into the land of Israel. (2 Kings 6:20b–23)

I think these are wonderful stories.

With healing the blind, it's possible we have the physical elements to it, but there are a lot of unanswered questions. However, I think the unanswered questions give us more evidence to the biblical tradition of miracles and miraculous healing of the blind.

What I would like for us to do now, is use the starting of this conference to let us be using the narrative of sight and light and recovery of sight and curing the blindness to go on and serve as our moral compass in this world.

Kimberly Curnyn
Presented at Garrett-Evangelical Theological Seminary
April 30, 2010

PART 4

Interfaith Community

11

Interfaith Futures in Academic and Religious Communities

A Panel Discussion

Philip Amerson, Morton Schapiro, Peter Knobel, Julie Windsor Mitchell, Souleymane Bachir Diagne, and Mark A. Dennis, Jr.

PRESIDENT AMERSON: MY NAME is Phil Amerson and I'm the president here at Garrett-Evangelical. One of the great joys of being in this post has been welcoming Morty Schapiro as the 16th president of Northwestern University. Morty and I have had a number of wonderful conversations and I think I understood better why he is able to be empathetic toward theological schools when I realized that he teaches a course in microeconomics—that certainly qualifies him to understand some of the limits we face in theology. It's also interesting that we're meeting on the same day that students are talking about sexuality and gender, and I understand that both have been wonderful conferences so far. The persons on this panel are folks we hope to engage and be in conversation with around their various faiths. You should know that when I met Dr. Schapiro, we talked a bit about his faith, and I invited him to join a group of local practitioners, leaders of faith communities here on the north shore. It was difficult, actually, to know who to invite and who not to invite, and we may want to do this again, maybe every year. But we promised to be following up together on the concern about inter-religious conversation, respect among faith communities, and what we might do. We brainstormed about it, and we thought we should do what we do best, and that is to hold conversations to bring academic and scholarly resources to bear on the question, and so it turned out that this event was a perfect occasion for us to continue the conversation. And we wanted to continue the conversation by inviting some local practitioners to be with us. Rev. Mark Dennis is pastor of Second Baptist Church here in Evanston; Peter Knobel is rabbi at Temple Beth Emet, and one of the things we need to be respectful of, by the way, is Shabbat coming up, so we can't go too long in our conversation. Julie Windsor Mitchell is campus pastor here at University Christian Ministry. Bachir is an imam who works with students and can help us understand another of the great Abrahamic traditions. I was on my way here today and realized that the gentleman driving the cab wasn't Christian—by all the postcards and things in his cab—but it turns out he was Ethiopian Orthodox, and it reminded me of the breadth of all of our traditions, that it's very difficult to even begin this conversation without a bit of humility that we represent just a small slice of each of our great traditions. I think Morty and I were going to start off by sharing our perspectives as leaders and our understanding of why interfaith sensitivity—more than dialogue—is important. I'm going to do three quick things before we engage the group, three things that come to mind as I sit in this place and try to do my work. The first comes from one of the great theologians of this school, a woman by the name of Georgia Harkness. We like to tell the story from this vantage point in a much more romantic fashion that I'm sure it actually occurred. We like to say that Georgia Harkness was the first full-time woman theologian to teach or be appointed to a theology school in the United States. That much is true. However, the sexism of the time meant that she was not a systematic theologian; she was appointed as an *applied* theologian, and the "boys" weren't willing to share the title of systematic theologian, even though she was a remarkable gift to the church and to the world. The chapel just to our south is where the 1954 gathering of the World Council of Churches was held, and the chapel was actually built and expanded for that meeting, the only time the World Council of Churches has met in the United States. There was a contest for poetry, and Georgia Harkness wrote a hymn that was the winner, and we still sing it, "Hope of the World." However, as her career was ending, Harkness was asked what her theological position was and, in an article in the *Christian Century*, she referred to herself as "a chastened liberal." What she meant by that was that the Second World War and the Holocaust had certainly modified her faith understanding, and her easy liberalism was no longer appropriate or even accessible. And so that's the first thing I want to share. That I think we do our work in this time—as a school that's had a reputation of being evangelical (in the European meaning of that word), for which piety is important, but a school that is very liberal and concerned with social justice—that we enter this 21st century as "chastened" liberals. And part of what that means is that we need to take very seriously, and with much humility, our role with regard to other religious traditions. The second thing I want to mention is that this institution increasingly needs to be a place of collaborative listening. I like to talk about it in terms of how students "audition"—from the Latin word *audire*, "to hear"—what professional schools do, provide a place to go to practice. And if we're not helping our students practice and learn to live in the interfaith realities of now and the future, then we're failing. And that's a piece of what I would want to talk about as collaborative listening. And, finally, I'm reluctant to use this word but I'll stick with it (George Bush has ruined it for me), but how about "compassionate living," living with a sense of compassion for others? Let me do a summation of this piece, and then I'll turn to Dr. Schapiro. He is so kind to come and enter a conversation around issues of faith, and I'm not in any way prepared to enter conversations about economics. I am so aware of the way we all think of ourselves as having expertise, and there's a quote I've lived with for a long time: "we are not human beings on a spiritual journey; we are spiritual beings on a human journey." And it seems to me that the more we can begin to be in tune with that, and know that all of our talents and expertise need to be reconceived and there needs to be a new "currency exchange" for how we understand our work, the better off we'll be. Those are some of the thing we wrestle with here at Garrett-Evangelical.

President Schapiro: The historical ties between Garrett and Northwestern are very strong, and now get to be even stronger, so I'm really excited about that. Phil mentioned that I've been president for eight months and I've done a lot of events, but I don't think anything was more interesting than the one on global clergy—that was a wonderful discussion. I don't know what the clergy expected, but we got into some pretty heavy discussions. The other thing Phil mentioned is that Garrett was hosting Chicago, all the different seminaries in this area, and Phil invited me there. That was interesting, because I do the economics of education, and I do a lot of work with loans, and pricing, and demographic change. I came to this really excited because I wanted to talk about God, and they wanted to talk about budgets. They could ask me about price strategies, and I could ask them about faith—so everyone was happy. It was a great discussion, and I learned so much and they learned a little. Northwestern is a great research university, and I love being its president. It's a *secular* research university. My whole professional career has been with secular, private universities and colleges, and sometimes, Phil, when you talk about the qualities you want Garrett graduates to have—including an abiding religious faith—in a way that is much harder for me to define in the secular world. I always define secular as does Tim, our fabulous chaplain, as being equally open to all faiths, not saying "no faith allowed," but holding all faiths. But a lot of private, secular education is not open to all faiths. It's always been a real challenge for me. I like being an economist, I like being a lot of things, but faith is number one—there's no question. I don't volunteer it unless people ask me, but they ask a lot. And I've had many occasions where I've asked to be a speaker for religious groups. The Muslim students, for example, invited me to have a wonderful discussion about the first-cousin relationship between Islam and Judaism. Catholics, you name it, everybody invites me, because they know I love to talk about it. But whenever I do, I don't exactly get in *trouble*, but I get people writing strong letters and emails to me. I had a wonderful hour and a half discussion with the Catholic folks at Sheil, and I learned so much, and of course, it was covered in the school paper, "President Schapiro shares his abiding religious faith." If you ask the faculty what's important for graduates, they'll say it's critical thinking skills, the ability to use data in a compelling way, public speaking, writing, love of learning, aesthetic sensibilities, and all. And I ask, "what about enhancing religious faith?" And people just look at me like I'm out of my mind. There was one piece that was actually very complimentary, but immediately the letters started coming. We have a wonderful group of secular humanists at Northwestern and I spoke to them, and the head of this organization wrote a very interesting letter to the *Daily* the next day and it said something like, it's okay to have a president who is deeply religious, but at Northwestern, there's no role for a religious president. And I couldn't quite get that, but I suppose it means that as long as I keep my faith in *shul*, it's okay because it somehow doesn't enter into my professional world. But it's there constantly—trust me—because it's who I am. It was a better reaction than when I wrote a column about "Bringing God to Williams College." That one I still get letters about. It's the world of academe. Sometimes I think that if I were at a religious institution, my life would be a little easier, but I like this challenge. A very heavily *endowed* religious institution, maybe. But count your blessings, thank you. But the truth is, I appreciate the challenge. I think that we could use more presidents at secular institutions asking these questions, and I've always liked to provoke people, so I get these discussions going. I think it's an important part of education. So I felt a little sorry for myself—every time I do this, it makes the press. But whenever you talk openly about these things, someone's going to be uncomfortable, particularly if you're the president of a very prominent, private, secular research university. So I felt sorry for myself but then in the last three weeks, I've done three events with a remarkable man named Francis Collins. Francis Collins is one of the great scientists in the world; he ran the Genome Project, won the Presidential Medal of Freedom, and now he runs the NIH. And Francis is a very, very religious Christian. I did three events with him recently, and I just read an interview with him and he basically said, "When you're one of the most visible scientists in the country, and you're very religious, they call you a religious nutcase and think it's really dangerous. And I'm advising the president. And yet I don't feel like I have to compartmentalize my role as a scientific advisor and my identity as a person of faith. And I think asking those questions—even though it doesn't solve it all, and even though it doesn't make people feel comfortable—I think it's important to use that pulpit I have as the president of the National Institutes of Health to remind people that God is in a place in my life that's above everything else." That's tough for Collins, because he's the head scientist. So if Francis Collins can be out there, I don't feel so sorry for myself. And I look forward to the discussion and learning from all of you. My professional expertise is economics, but I've got this hobby that really excites me more than anything else in my life.

President Amerson: Why don't I just open it up to any of you up front to jump in, say what you like, and help us with this conversation.

Rabbi Knobel: I think it's exciting to have a president of a great secular university, this is important to me. Having taught at a number of significant academic institutions and knowing the hostility that exists in some of them, it certainly is great to see this. Obviously, most of us are concerned that the classroom is not an opportunity for proselytizing or for people who honestly express difference. I had a very wonderful experience teaching in college more than 30 years ago. I had two interesting courses, and one was on Jewish-Christian relations, and that was with the chairman of the department who was a practicing Episcopal priest, as well as an academic. It was clear that both of us were people of faith, both of us had serious Ph.D.s from serious secular institutions. And, at the same time, we were able not only to talk about our own religions but to offer concerns and critiques with respect to the religion of the other and comment on how historically they had related to each other. The second experience that I had was the opportunity to teach a course in Christianity, and I think that one of the things that helps us to better understand the other—when you're forced to teach about the other's faith. And that goes also when one teaches about the diversity *within* one's own faith. Can one be honest about the disagreements one has with members of one's own religious community, but present their positions fairly? The other thing I would say is that many of my most important experiences have been with other clergy who have been honest in their faith and shared their faith with me. One is Bob Thompson and the other was David Handley. Each of them comes from a very different position, but our relationship was built not on tolerance, it was built on respect, real conversations, and real work. In that regard, you learn much more about who you are and what you ought to believe. So, when I've had the opportunity to teach at a secular institution, I've allowed students to make judgments about statements I make, and I also ask them to challenge me if the things I'm saying ultimately are unfair. We then have those wonderful opportunities. The other thing for me is outside the classroom, when students have had the opportunity to come to me not necessarily as a professor but as a person of faith, so they can talk about the challenges of their own faiths.

Dr. Diagne: Something you said reminded me of the first president of Senegal. Senegal is a country that is 95 percent Muslims, four percent Catholics, and one percent traditional African religions. Léopold Sédar Senghor was the first president and he was Catholic, in a predominantly Muslim country. He once wrote a piece similar to what you say, about having to do the budget but thinking about God. He wrote, "I know tomorrow Senegal's parliament is meeting, and this is obviously very important, but I just don't feel like going. I'm preoccupied with the question of God at this point, I want rather to read Father Pierre Teilhard de Chardin. Because God is the question that is always posed." And, when he was saying that, he was quoting Karl Marx. Whenever I think of this man we had for our first president, someone who belonged to such a small minority (almost nonexistent) in a Muslim country, I think of his understanding of secular. How, in a strictly secular country, the kind of secular country he was trying to build, the rule for faith is profound belief. At the same, he believed the best way to organize a state was to draw on the existing capacity he saw in faith to still be at work in the nation. That is the kind of vision he tried to have for his country as he built it as the first president. And I always think of the case of Senegal, and when it comes to making sure God has the room he has to have. The second reaction I have to what you say, and talking about my hope, is that somehow I have discovered my own faith through interfaith dialogue. I was raised a Muslim, and I belonged to a family where I realized afterwards somehow that my father was very efficient in feeding me with things that I didn't realize he was feeding me with. He always taught me many things, but at the same time, left me alone. He did not interfere with my practice. The first time I left, I was 17, and I went to the *université/lycée* and I was supposed to be in the dorm but there was no room, so a few of us had to stay at another place. And I stayed with this man who said he was Iranian but also Nigerian. I asked as politely if I could if we could pray together, and then I asked if he was Muslim. He said yes, but in a different way, and I'll explain after we pray. So, after the prayer, he said that he was actually Baha'i. So I asked him why he said he was Muslim, and he said, if you had asked me if I were Christian, I also would have said "yes." So you can see that with premises like that, you can have an infinite conversation. And my friendship with him brought me to ask myself what faith meant for me, and I think that was very much for the first time. What it meant for me to be a Muslim, and this is how I started examining everything I had been learning in my life, sucking in without really thinking about it. So the notion he had as a Baha'i, that his religion was about being the "religion of religions" and reconciling different faiths, made our conversation a kind of interfaith conversation.

Rev. Mitchell: As I've been thinking about the context I work in at Northwestern, I work in a secular institution but I do *ministry* in a secular institution, but which makes it a peculiar type of ministry and a difficult problem. I'm sure all of the clergy on campus would explain the way they wrestle with this dilemma in different ways. We have a lot of very wonderful religious and lively religious communities on campus, but students come from a lot of different religious backgrounds and some from no religious background—so it's difficult to try to do ministry that reaches everyone. It's in fact not possible. You need different communities to do ministry for different populations. As a result, the way that I've done that over the last several years is to try to reach out to students who often come from a Christian background but maybe a fairly secular Christian background, usually the liberal Protestant Christian sort. But many of those students don't have strong religious identities that come from their home backgrounds, so what that means is that in many ways, I'm doing interfaith work all the time. Let me give you an example. At UCM, we have five students living there. Right now, we have a Chinese, international student who is a very new Christian. We have an Episcopalian, one who is definitely, unashamedly atheist and wants to talk about that, a Muslim student, and a United Methodist. That right there is our little interfaith dialogue that happens literally every single day at UCM. There are all kinds of other dialogues and events with various speakers to try and lift up all of these issues around spirituality. The thing that would resonate with students is what you said, Phil, about us being spiritual beings on a human journey—that's where a lot of Northwestern students are in terms of their faith. I'm always trying to find new ways to tap into that very deep longing in students for some real intentional religious dialogue, which touches the core of who they are, their real true identities. Of course, this is part of college, figuring out what that identity is. So part of it is simply a developmental issue. But let me also say that I'm adjunct faculty here at Garrett, so I bridge the institutions you two are talking about. Given the fact that the reality I work in every day is an interfaith context, when I work with M.Div. students here at Garrett, many of them aren't familiar with doing ministry in that kind of context. So I've had many conversations with students over the last few years I've been teaching here, about how to do ministry in an interfaith world. And I don't know if I should admit this, but one day, we organized a trip to the Baha'i Temple. There was one student from Northwestern who graduated last year who was very active in UCM and now works at the Baha'i Temple and gives tours there. She feels a part of that community and is comfortable there, so I took my group from Garrett and had this wonderful dialogue there about what it means to do ministry in an interfaith context. I think that's very important for seminary students to think about that process, because that's the reality of the university and it's also the reality for all of us who are doing ministry every single day.

Rev. Dennis: There's a quiet, fervent, strong group of people who live on the north shore, and included in that group are Rev. Bob Thompson, Rabbi Peter Knobel, and many other clergy in the area. It's not a revival of the civil right movement, not a green movement, not a movement around immigration—we're still trying to define it, and our quest is to find, as Howard Thurman describes, our common ground. And I think that's important. There is in our tradition a phrase, a *kairos* moment, a moment when God intervenes in human history. And I think that there is a *kairos* moment that's happening in this community, and that doesn't mean it's not happening in other communities, but I think you are seeing a movement by God in a way that none of us can explain. This president is here for a reason, and I think it's not only noble, but a godsend to have a president who says "I'm a man of faith," and doesn't mind what people say. I think it's wonderful to have Phil Amerson as the president of Garrett, who comes to the table with many different experiences. And the two of them are joining together. It's a moment in time when this institution is being called to address the plethora of social problems. I come from a perspective that refuses to be locked into a box, I only hire people who have a passion and can build a niche rather than looking for cubbyholes. There is something about the urge, the drive to want to be free, and there is a song out of the spiritual tradition says, "Have you got good religion?" And the response is, "Certainly, certainly, certainly, Lord." And I've thought about that many different ways, and I think that is the resounding question going around that we're all being tested and asking, "What is the meaning of interfaith? What is the meaning of pluralism? What is the meaning of trying to come together as a community of one?" Good religion, to me, does not mean you stand totally and firmly on the faith that was given to you by your ancestors, but it is the affirmation of a God who is able to be bigger than the box you put God in. It means that God is not the problem, and not necessarily the solution, but our task is given to work together through collaboration, communications, and the struggle to find the answer—and that in itself becomes the solution to many of our problems. Healthcare is terrible—sorry, Mr. President. I'm getting sick and tired of going to the hospital and buying more medicines and not finding a cure. But whether you like the healthcare bill or not, we are now in a conversation about what it means to have quality health care. Before, we stayed away from it; we were afraid of the politics associated with it. But now, our parents are older, and we need to talk about their care. I think we've been divinely forced into a conversation about how we bridge the divide among us, not just here in America, but globally. The sooner we learn how to work across the Atlantic and Pacific and see that we are truly one community, our faith will be stronger, but not in the same way we've known traditionally. That's a major change in our society. I think this is a *kairos* moment, coming with this university, this seminary, many of the people in this community to have this conversation. I'm reminded of Benjamin Mays, who got his Ph.D. from the University of Chicago. Right before he finished there, he wrote a book entitled *Disturbed about Man*, and in that book, he raised different questions. One of them was this: "I'm disturbed about man, not because we don't have the educational facilities for people to learn, to increase their cognition; I'm concerned about man, not because we don't have the economics in place to help people get better in this capitalist society." And he went on and on. He said, "I'm concerned about man because we're failing to teach that which builds character." And character, in our society, comes from corporate America. Values dictate the hate. If we were ever to have a conversation about values across interfaith lines, the values that would ensure ethical behavior, the good of all communities, I think we will find the answer we've been searching for. If it is true that values affect behavior, organizationally, in community, and individually, we might be on to the answer the whole world is searching for. If that's the case, my question is: "what would it look like for an institution like Northwestern University and the Garrett-Evangelical seminaries of the world, to be leaders in shaping better global character and communication across denomination and in education?" Have you got good religion? I'd like for that answer to be, "certainly."

President Philip Amerson: Can you keep your questions brief?

Question from group: I'm still trying to get my mind around the fact that the president of Northwestern University sitting in this space. Historically, it's been otherwise. But you're not just here, you're sitting here comfortably, engaging in the dialogue. Because of your open affirmation of faith at this secular university, can you say whether the university encourages the teaching of intelligent design, evolution, or whatever? How does a faithful president of a secular university get at the larger issues faced in education around that issue? The other question Rev. Dennis prompted in me involves how a university president facilitates the building of character in students?

President Schapiro: Teaching for character . . . you always think that if you expose people to world dilemmas, you'll get them to think about values. In fact, one of the courses I'm teaching next year is about ethics and values and we'll spend some time grappling with world dilemmas and we'll do this in the context of social science policy, which I'm much more familiar with. And I think that also sort of addresses your first question. I can teach economics, and I do apply econometrics, but I can apply it to questions about social justice, questions about universal health coverage, or questions about raising the minimum wage. So I don't know how I do my job differently in terms of how I teach. I do have something to say, although most college presidents don't set the curriculum, but we can weight it, sometimes subtly. If you're too overt, particularly if you're out of the mainstream, there can be a backlash. You get to convene a lot of discussions, working with the chaplains, I get to support dialogue, support various programs and efforts. If there was ever any hesitancy about the willingness to raise certain questions, in fact, I'm out there in the dorms every week, and it gives them some cover, makes it even more possible to have those discussions. Francis Collins is asked all the time, "What do you think about stem-cell research? What do you think about abortion?" and this and that, and he says, "I don't know, I don't know if I can separate that really. But this is who I am, and I want to be a positive role-model." So I try not to let my faith stop discussions, but encourage them.

Question from group: One of the biggest problems I faced in medicine was disciplinary turf and, of course, I had a terrible time facilitating departmental dialogue deeper than surface level, so now we throw in interfaith. What lessons have you learned from the academic side about how to navigate different religious turfs?

President Amerson: This may or may not touch that, but I think it gets at it. I had to fly back to Evanston today because I was meeting in another place. Those of you who have been following what's going on in the Methodist Church will know that we've got a seminary claiming that it's going to become the first interfaith United Methodist seminary. What's fascinating about that is the imposition of the language. It also goes back to talking about Northwestern being a secular university. And this school is in the Los Angeles area, and it's not so simple, because when you start making these alliances, you include one Jewish community and you leave out another. You include one Muslim community, and you leave out another. And what about the Latter Day Saints? And all of this is done sometimes with a sense of arrogance that we're out on the forefront, when in fact, all of our schools are wrestling in one way of another with how we have different voices and how we move beyond not just the disciplines but also the traditions and have a wider, more respectful conversation. If you know Los Angeles, you know that as soon as you pick one Jewish congregation and not another, that's a problem. That's true with other traditions, too. So that's some of what I wrestle with. It's not just the narrowness of the departments, but it's also these other issues. That's a piece of the dilemma.

Rev. Stephens: One thing I was thinking about during the discussion is the fact that about five years ago, we did a survey of graduate students at Northwestern. We were interested to know what students' perceptions were of spirituality on campus; we were interested in these questions. So we especially asked, "Do you want to have faculty discussing their own religious perspectives, in a variety of settings in the classroom, in office hours, in a fireside discussions?" What was gratifying is that students gave a nuanced answer, which is, "there are times when it's not appropriate. If it's a calculus class, we don't care. But in other courses, for faculty to talk about their own perspective would be welcomed." So I think the time is right for these conversations, and the hard work is to figure out how to go about that, how to be inviting, and set appropriate boundaries. I think it's a conversation they want to have, whether they're particularly religious or not. Courses in our religion department are always oversubscribed, and what I hear from students is, "I can take a course on Christianity, Hinduism, Buddhism, whatever, and it's a safe place for me to raise crucial questions in my life, but not in a way that people will start praying about me or in a way that's intrusive." There's lots of evidence that students are really eager to have those conversations and the question is, "will we respond?" I think we will. How are we going to respond in a way that's appropriate and helpful? One last observation: you were talking about interfaith dialogue, and I don't want to move too quickly past that, because I think there are important questions to be raised about that. For all the questions and complexities about interfaith dialogue, it beats the heck out of interfaith violence. We live in a dangerous world, and a world in which we are increasingly rubbing up against each other. I think that by addressing these issues on our campus, we have a real opportunity to change the world. Because our students are going to go out and be leaders, and they'll take the values they pick up that we display for them. I know this is happening; we've had an interfaith organization on our campus for the past 15 years or so, and a student dropped by last spring and she's working in a not-for-profit in the Bay Area, and she's a musician. She was the very first president of our interfaith organization, and she said, "Of all the things I experienced at Northwestern as an undergraduate, that was the one thing that helped me to do the work I'm doing today. I learned about a world of difference and how to construct a conversation." It's work that's going to pay off, and it's important, and I am encouraged about the emerging opportunities.

Rabbi Knobel: Often, when we get in these conversations, I think about a passage from the *Talmud*—and I think both the passage and the *Talmudic* methodology itself can be helpful to us as we talk about the interfaith conversation. It's "these and these are the words of the living God." So whether, for example, Pastor Dennis or I totally agree on the nature of a God, when I hear Pastor Dennis talk about his faith and how God moves him, I make the assumption that this is a legitimate expression of God's will and that enables me to hear it in a different way. And it enables us to reach a level of discussion that is important. The second thing about *Talmudic* method is that it's a method of asking questions, asking for constant clarification: "What do you really mean by this? What are the implications?" It seems to me that when you have real conversations—the "audition," when you really listen—you can have the most productive conversations with people who fundamentally disagree with you. For example, I'm now involved in a dialogue at Wheaton College. And you can imagine that the difference between Reform Judaism and Wheaton College is significant, but one of the most interesting things about that dialogue is that half of the professors sitting in that room are graduates of my seminary, the Hebrew Union College. We had a conversation a few months ago about the Sermon on the Mount, and I argued from my perspective about this being a passage that clearly indicated Jesus as the Moses figure, the law-giver meant to replace Moses. The young man with a Ph.D. from Hebrew Union College argued on the basis of *Talmud* and *Mishnah* and all of the classic Jewish texts. And it was a fascinating conversation because it is very clear to all of us in the room that every one of those professors would love us to find Jesus, but those conversations are truly important because they are honest and open and it creates a community of faith, which is different from the kind of mealy-mouthed "all of us are the same" kind of community. By the way, one of my least favorite phrases lately is the "Abrahamic faiths." It's a phrase that's meant to cover up certain kinds of significant differences. But it seems to me that if we can learn, whether it's in the academic or the religious community, that when it comes to these very important cross-religion, cross-community, cross-disciplinary kinds of conversations, to really hear and listen to each other and understand the inherent truth behind them without trying to become a relativist. What happens is you change the dynamic, and when you change the dynamic, you can move to something I would never have said before I met Pastor Dennis, is move toward the beloved community. I'm learning to talk like a Protestant. The important thing about this conversation, about both Phil and Morty here is to say that faith has an important place in the important institutions that are designed to help prepare us to be the kind of society we want to be. One of the best way to teach values is through the way in which we behave and I'm still a real believer that when leaders in any field behave in ways that represent respect and integrity, it transforms the community they lead, and it gives us the faith to be honest with ourselves. I want to personally thank Phil and Morty for doing this and for encouraging these kinds of conversations, because I believe this is terribly important.

President Schapiro: I learn a lot in these kinds of discussions. Out of respect for one another, we listen more carefully. We do share the same values, even if we don't share the same God. And to say that we all share the same God—I used to say that, but I never say it anymore. Because in fact, I don't think we share the same God. We can still identify with the values, and have a very good conversation without watering down our beliefs. This is an important step forward. I love the title, "God as Light," because that's something we can all embrace—light leading us toward truth, justice. I feel very blessed; I moved to this community last summer and never found a more welcoming religious community. People are asking these questions in a very honest and open way, and I haven't generally seen that. Talk about being truly blessed: we share our campus with Garrett, and that's just an absolute privilege for Northwestern.

Dr. Philip Amerson
President, Professor of Sociology of Religion
Garrett-Evangelical Theological Seminary

Dr. Morton Schapiro
President, Professor of Management and Strategy
Northwestern University

Rabbi Peter S. Knobel
Rabbi, Beth Emet The Free Synagogue
Evanston

Rev. Julie Windsor Mitchell
University Christian Ministry
Northwestern University

Rev. Mark A. Dennis, Jr.
Senior Pastor, Second Baptist Church of Evanston

Dr. Souleymane Bachir Diagne
Professor of French, Director of Graduate Studies
Columbia University

Panel Discussion
Garrett-Evangelical Theological Seminary

April 30, 2010

Contributors

Philip Amerson

Philip Amerson, President and Professor of Sociology of Religion at Garrett-Evangelical Theological Seminary, was previously president and professor of church and society at The Claremont School of Theology. He also has served as a faculty member at Butler University, Christian Theological Seminary, Asbury Seminary, Candler School of Theology, and Westmont College. An ordained Methodist pastor, President. Amerson has been a delegate to the General Conference of the UMC and currently is Director of the General Board of Higher Education and Ministry.

Jamal Badawi

A highly sought-after lecturer, Dr. Jamal Badawi has been one of the best-known Muslim speakers in the West for more than two decades. Born and raised in Egypt, Badawi received his bachelor's degree from Ain Shams University in Cairo. He then moved to the U.S. and attended Indiana University, where he earned both his master's and doctoral degrees in Business Administration. After teaching a course on Islam at Stanford University, Badawi went on to become a professor at Saint Mary's University in Halifax, Nova Scotia (Canada), in the Departments of Religious Studies and Management. Badawi is the Director of the Halifax-based Islamic Information Foundation, a non-profit that strives to promote a better understanding of Islam by both Muslims and non-Muslims. Badawi also is a member of the Council of North America, the Islamic Society of North America, the Consultative Council of North America, and the Juristic Council of North America. He is also a Board member of the Council on American-Islamic Relations.

Kimberley Curnyn

Kimberley M. Curnyn, M.D. is Clinical Professor in Pediatric Ophthalmology at the University of Illinois Medical Center. Dr. Curnyn has taught on ethical issues in biology and medicine and serves on the board of directors of the Chicago Clinical Ethics Program. In addition to lecturing regularly to ophthalmology residents on various topics, she has spoken on a wide range of subjects, including ethical and legal concerns, responsibilities of healthcare providers, and women's health issues. Dr. Curnyn also has a private practice in ophthalmology and is active in medical missions and is founding clinics around the world.

Mark A. Dennis, Jr.

Rev. Dennis is Senior Pastor of Second Baptist Church of Evanston in Evanston, Illinois. Before becoming pastor of Second Baptist Church, Rev. Dennis served as a gifted leader of numerous congregations across the country. He also has worked in higher education and the non-profit sector, serving as adjunct lecturer at such institutions as The University of Chicago and DePaul University. He is the recipient of several awards—including the Benjamin Franklin Award for "The Best Professional Leader in Philanthropy"—and is a frequent speaker and facilitator for churches, professional associations, and institutions of higher education. Pastor Dennis currently serves on the boards of North Park University, The Milton Murray Foundation for Philanthropy, The Church and the Black Experience, Garrett-Evangelical Theological Seminary, and Metropolitan Family Services of Evanston.

Souleymane Bachir Diagne

Souleymane Bachir Diagne is Professor of French and Director of Graduate Studies at Columbia University. Dr. Diagne teaches in many fields, including Islamic philosophy, African philosophy, and literature. He is the author of , as well as several other books on Islamic and African philosophy. He has a particular interest in early modern philosophy, philosophy and Sufism in the Islamic world, African philosophy and literature, philosophy of science, and 20th-century French philosophy.

Wendy Doniger

Wendy Doniger is the Mircea Eliade Distinguished Service Professor of the History of Religions at the University of Chicago Divinity School. Dr.

Doniger also teaches in the Department of South Asian Languages and Civilizations. Her research and teaching interests revolve around two basic areas: Hinduism and mythology. Among her many books published are three Penguin Classics: *Hindu Myths: A Sourcebook, Translated from the Sanskrit*; *The Rig Veda: An Anthology,* 108 *Hymns Translated from the Sanskrit*; and *The Laws of Manu*.

Peter Knobel

Rabbi Peter S. Knobel has been the spiritual leader of Beth Emet The Free Synagogue in Evanston, Illinois since 1980. In addition to his congregational responsibilities, Rabbi Knobel serves in leadership roles in the Reform movement on a national level as well as being actively involved in the Chicago-area community. Rabbi Knobel is past president of the Chicago Board of Rabbis and the Chicago Association of Reform Rabbis and is active in the Evanston Downtown Clergy Association and a member of the Board of the Council of the Parliament of World Religions. He is a member of the National Interreligious Leadership Initiative on Peace in the Middle East. Rabbi Knobel has taught extensively at a number of colleges including HUC-JIR, Yale University, Connecticut College, and Spertus Institute, on subjects ranging from Biblical Aramaic to Jewish mysticism to Israel in Christian thought and Jewish Bioethics. He also has authored and edited numerous articles and publications in the areas of Jewish Bioethics, Liturgy, and Zionist Thought.

Larry Murphy

Larry Murphy is a Professor of the History of Christianity at Garrett-Evangelical Theological Seminary. He has a passion for pointing students to the story behind the story, to the complex, multi-layered dynamics of human interaction in community—enabling them to see the figures of history as real individuals wresting with issues of life and love, identity, security, and destiny within the heritage of the Judeo-Christian tradition. Dr. Murphy received his bachelor's degree from Michigan State University and his Ph.D. from Graduate Theological Union. He is the author of numerous journal articles, a contributor to the Encyclopedia of World Religions, the author of *African-American Faith in America*, and the editor of *Down by the Riverside: Readings in African-American Religion*.

William Murphy

William Murphy is a Lecturer in the Department of Anthropology at Northwestern University. Dr. Murphy has taught on a wide range of subjects, including language and culture, law and culture, and selected topics in anthropology. His research interests include language, culture, politics, the anthropology of violence, youth and culture practice, and Liberia and Sierra Leone, West Africa.

Yohanan Petrovsky-Shtern

Yohanan Petrovsky-Shtern is an Associate Professor of Jewish History and Director of the Crown Family Center of Jewish Studies at Northwestern University. He teaches Early Modern, Modern, and East European Jewish history and culture, Jewish Mysticism and Kabbalah, and Slavic-Jewish Literatures. In 2009, he received a Northwestern University Distinguished Teaching Award. He has published more than a hundred articles and authored three books.

Morton Schapiro

Morton Schapiro, President of Northwestern University, is a Professor of Economics in the Weinberg College of Arts and Sciences and also holds appointments in the Kellogg School of Management and School of Education and Social Policy. President Schapiro is among the nation's leading authorities on the economics of higher education. He has testified before U.S. Senate and House committees on economic and educational issues and is widely quoted in the national media on those issues. President Schapiro has written more than 100 articles and five books.

Jan Van Eys

Jan Van Eys is Clinical Professor Emeritus of Pediatrics at Vanderbilt University Medical School and Senior Scholar of the Center for Biomedical Ethics and Public Policy.

Kenneth L. Vaux

Kenneth L. Vaux, Professor of Theology and Ethics at Garrett-Evangelical Theological Seminary, is a member of the Graduate Faculty at Northwestern University and Fellow of the Centre for Advanced Religious and Theological Studies (CARTS) at Cambridge. He is the author of more than 200 articles, newspaper essays, books reviews, and juried papers. He also has written or edited more than 20 books.

Sara Anson Vaux

Sara Vaux is a Lecturer in the Department of Religion at Northwestern University. She has taught on religion, literature, and film at the University of Chicago, Garrett-Evangelical Theological Seminary, North Park Seminary, and Northwestern University since 1998. Dr. Vaux has written on the arts and issues in ethics, including *Finding Meaning at the Movies*, co-author of *Dying Well in the Late Twentieth Century*; "Suffering and Healing in Films," *Christianity and the Arts*, and editor and contributor to *Working Well: Business Ethics*. Her forthcoming book explores theology in the films of Clint Eastwood.

Richard Vaux

Richard Vaux is a Landscape and Lightscape Artist whose work is represented in hundreds of galleries, public and private collections, one-man shows, exhibitions, and publications throughout the U.S., Canada, South America, Europe, and the Far East. He "creates shapes that are sometimes pure abstraction, and other times forms that strongly suggest landscape features . . . his meditations on nature, while not overtly religious, convey the immanence of the sacred."

Julie Windsor Mitchell

Rev. Julie Windsor Mitchell is the chaplain in charge of University Christian Ministry at Northwestern University. An ordained minister in the United Church of Christ, she is a graduate of Brown University, with a major in religious studies. She received her Master of Divinity from Harvard Divinity School, where she worked with students at the Harvard Chapel. Prior to coming to Northwestern, Rev. Mitchell was pastor of St. John's United Church of Christ for four years.

K.K. Yeo

K.K. Yeo is Harry R. Kendall Professor of New Testament Studies at Garrett-Evangelical Theological Seminary, Visiting Professor in the Philosophy and Religious Studies Department and Academic Director of the Christian Studies program at Peking University. He has served as an advisory member of the Graduate School Faculty of Northwestern

University. His teaching and research have centered on culture and the Bible, especially New Testament and Chinese cultures in the context of global biblical interpretation. He is the author of more than 100 articles and conference papers, as well as more than 20 books, including *Musing With Confucius and Paul: Toward a Chinese Christian Theology* and *The Spirit Intercedes: The New Testament in Prayers and Images* (with Claire Matheny).

www.ingramcontent.com/pod-product-compliance
Lightning Source LLC
Chambersburg PA
CBHW051949160426
43198CB00013B/2377